Loeb Classical Monographs

in memory of James C. Loeb

Euripides
and the
Full Circle
of Myth

Cedric H. Whitman

Harvard University Press
Cambridge, Massachusetts

1974

The Loeb Classical Monographs
are published with assistance
from the Loeb Classical Library Foundation

Library of Congress Catalog Card Number 74–81676

ISBN 0–674–26920–9

Printed in the United States of America

Preface

The art of Euripides is so varied, so given to the unexpected, that it is no wonder that all attempts at a consistent, general theory of his work have failed to carry conviction. It is almost a commentary on himself, as well as on human life, that he closed no less than five plays with identical choral lines stressing the unforeseeable, as if even he was not quite sure what he would do next. Euripides has had more labels attached to him than any other dramatist who ever lived, none in the least helpful save insofar as their sum provides an index to the poverty of one-sided critical views of a poet capable of everything except one-sidedness. The ambivalence of his earliest critic, Aristophanes, is clear throughout the comedies; and the purport of his earliest extant tragedy, the *Alcestis,* is still, after nearly two and a half millennia, highly debatable. It was natural, perhaps, for his contemporaries to be astonished, shocked, or even enchanted by Euripides, and then give Sophocles the prize. It was natural too, though not a sign of heightened critical acuity, for the fourth and later centuries to adopt Euripides to their special liking; presumably he seemed at once more accessible and more philosophic. But from the time when Aristotle called him the most tragic of the poets to the present, when it is becoming fashionable to search out his affinities with the comic, there has appeared no broad interpretive scheme competent to contain the full range of his labyrinthine imagination.

Certainly this essay offers nothing of the sort. It was written primarily out of the wish to formulate a somewhat personal reading of three plays that have always aroused controversy as well as admiration. The *Iphigeneia in Tauris*, a long-standing favorite, the *Ion*, a little neglected until lately, and above all the "bewundert viel und viel gescholten" *Helen* have undergone widely divergent interpretations. Yet, by contrast with what was said above about the diversity of Euripides' work, these three dramas have much in common with each other, though little that is obvious with the rest of the corpus. On internal grounds all seem to have been written around the year 412 B.C., the fixed date of the *Helen*; all have striking similarities in dramatic form and content, including the so-called happy endings which account for such designations as "romance," "tragicomedy," and "melodrama." In addition, they possess a certain community of theme, less often noticed, but crucial to the meaning of that final act of salvation by which the endings are called happy. This theme is the quest for purity, or wholeness. It finds itself through a complex of intricately woven poetic motifs, the sea, music, a branch of olive; but it is the struggle for wholeness, for spiritual, not merely physical, redemption that gives these plays their relative coherence as a special segment of Euripides' work.

In order to make the book available to all those interested in Greek tragedy, I have translated extracts, and transliterated certain key words, leaving only a few necessarily in Greek. Also, there are no notes. Some scholars might consider a book without notes quite as useless as one without pictures and conversations, but they seemed burdensome, since classicists at work on Euripides will know what they might have said, while others would probably skip them. It seemed sufficient to compile a brief list of selected books and articles that I found relevant. One of these, Charles Segal's "The Two

Worlds of Euripides' *Helen*," was written simultaneously with my chapter, and quite independently of it. Our views about this difficult play have a great deal in common, even to the comparison with *Cymbeline*; but for the sake of the total argument I have let my chapter stand as written, while earnestly referring the reader to the more detailed treatment in Segal's article.

This book was begun under a grant from the James C. Loeb Foundation during the year 1969–70, while I was on sabbatical leave from Harvard; I am more than usually indebted also to friends, students, and fellow scholars for their encouragement and help in bringing it to completion. From the beginning, my wife, Anne, listened with patience and reassuring support to the entire book, as its various parts were written. Maud Wilcox and Margaretta Fulton, of the Harvard University Press, also read the manuscript even before it was officially submitted for publication. Among students with whom I have worked directly on Euripides, I should name Rowland Hazard and Justina Gregory, whose respective studies of the *Hecuba* and of madness in the *Heracles*, *Orestes*, and *Bacchae* have considerably furthered my own thinking about those plays. Also, I extend warm thanks to Laura Slatkin and David Kovacs for their careful critical readings and many valuable suggestions, both scholarly and stylistic. Finally, I must acknowledge my debt to Anne Pippin Burnett who generously, and despite our differing outlooks, offered many helpful comments; and to C. J. Herington, whose compelling critical imperium not only eliminated a number of lapses from the first three of these essays, but also effectively brought about, *inopinata vi*, the existence of the fourth.

Greensboro, Vermont   C.H.W.
August 1973

Contents

For what you lost was but a rose
That flowered and failed through nature's gift;
Now, by this kind of chest enclosed,
It is found a pearl whose price is proved;
And you have charged your fate with theft.

THE PEARL

1

Iphigeneia
in Tauris

Artemis is one of the most self-contradictory divinities in the Olympian pantheon. Though she is a huntress, she is also Mistress of Animals and protects them, especially when young. One of her Homeric epithets, "Arrow-scatterer," associates her with the wilds in a somewhat masculine role; another, "Of the golden distaff," connotes the utmost in feminine domesticity. Herself a virgin, she is a patroness of virgins, in fact of youth in general; on the other hand, she slays them, and is accountable for any sudden, painless death of women. Though normally conceived of as tall and of striking beauty, whence her epithet "Most Fair," yet she seems, at Brauron at least, to have been identified with a bear, and the story of Callisto implies the same. For all her virginity, she is a fertility goddess who presides over childbirth, whence, as Pausanias notes (II, 35, 1), she has the epithet Iphigeneia. And although, like her brother, she cannot defile herself with the sight of death, she can require human sacrifice. Anthropologically speaking, these contradictions are simply the result of various local identifications with other goddesses; but logically and theologically, puzzles arise of the kind that captivated Euripides' imagination on many occasions. For though his characters often remonstrate openly with the gods and criticize them, his purpose in exploiting their baffling and contrary actions was not, as some critics have thought, to deride and reject the divinities of myth, but rather to plumb their mysteries and to frame his own perspective. The *Iphigeneia* does, of course, make use of all the devices that were later to become the furniture of New Comedy—long-lost people, recognition, intrigue—but it also maintains a high degree of concern for the nature and meaning of the gods, as do all three romances. There is melodrama, but there is also theology. Less symbolic than the *Helen* in its treatment of divinity, and less laden than the *Ion* with divinely sent human suffering, the *Iphigeneia* is nonetheless centered upon the problems of Olympian behavior and its relation to attainable truth.

The form of the story adopted by Euripides starts with a contradiction: Artemis demands the sacrifice of Iphigeneia at Aulis and then rescues her victim and transports her to the land of the Taurians in the Crimea. Agamemnon's vow, to sacrifice to Artemis the fairest thing born in a certain year, was a vow of sacrifice for safe return, a familiar motif that has parallels in Idomeneus, Jephtha, and others. The "fairest thing" turned out to be Iphigeneia, but Agamemnon seems to have forgotten until the host was mustered at Aulis. Neither Aeschylus nor Sophocles mentions any such vow; they give different reasons for the wrath of Artemis, and there is, of course, no reprieve. Iphigeneia's story accords well with Euripides' lifelong obsession with early death and youthful martyrs. But his Iphigeneia does not meet with actual death; by miracle she is saved, and miraculous salvation is quite in the spirit of the romances. The tale of Iphigeneia among the Taurians would then be a kind of archetype for Euripides' motivating instincts in these three plays, a tale of divine power roused and active, but somehow stayed; of tragedy suffered, but rounded into peace. His rendering of it emerges as one of the most meticulously constructed and poetically vivid of all surviving Greek plays.

The prologue has two parts, Iphigeneia's monologue and the scene between Orestes and Pylades. Since the main action of the play is to bring together two persons who believe each other to be dead, it is suggestive to stage both at the very opening, but without letting them meet: such a device, possibly first used by Sophocles in his *Electra*, powerfully motivates and underscores the dramatic structure of the whole. Iphigeneia's speech begins in the usual "playbill" manner as she sets the scene, identifies herself, and relates her supposed sacrifice at Aulis, how she was lured there by a promise of marriage to Achilles, then spirited away by Artemis to the land of the Taurians to become her priestess in human sacrifices. Up to this point the tone has been matter-of-fact, but at line 42 one detects a change, as Iphigeneia narrates her dream to the purifying aether. The relation between the lines and their constituent clauses becomes more irregular, while the shifting subjects of the infinitives produce a certain jerkiness, and asyndeton and frequent enjambements quicken the pace:

> I thought in sleep that, parted from this land,
> I dwelt in Argos, and among my maids
> Lay sleeping, but the back of earth rolled quaking,
> And I arose and fled outside and saw
> The palace copestone falling, and the whole roof
> Stricken in ruins from pillar tops to floor.
> One only column in my dream was left
> Of the ancestral hall, and from its cap
> Let down gold locks, and took a human voice,
> And I, honoring this rite I have of slaying
> Strangers, sprinkled him as one death-devoted,
> Weeping.   (44–55)

The tremulously emotional tone challenges translation, but is marked in the Greek. Such imitations of "voice-ways," to use Reuben Brower's term in his book on Robert Frost, are anything but characteristic of tragic speech. The language of tragedy as established by Aeschylus and refined by Sophocles is lofty, remote, and severe, designed to convey thoughts and emotions through words and images, but little concerned with subtle vocal tonality. By and large Euripides kept to this tradition, though throughout his career he progressively loosened the iambic trimeter and divested it of its massiveness. His aim seems to have been to achieve immediacy rather than actual realism. But in the three romances, and especially in the *Iphigeneia*, the voices become audible as voices; much of the time one hears not only what is said but how it is said, in a way seldom known to earlier tragedy.

Iphigeneia misinterprets her dream, rather surprisingly, to the effect that Orestes is dead. The one standing pillar should have indicated the opposite, but she takes her performance of presacrificial, lustral rites as token of his doom. Actually, the dream has stated, though in symbolic terms, the situation of the play. The contrast between ambiguous dreams and clear truth is thematic, and becomes the subject of a singular and striking ode later on (1234 ff); but the contrast is not developed as it will be in the *Helen*, where it forms a philosophic core, a central paradox amid the depths and recesses of universal illusion. It is one-dimensional in the *Iphigeneia*, and consists of no more than dispelling a misapprehension in the mind of each of the two main characters. Once that is done and the truth revealed, there remains only the problem of how to act upon it.

When Iphigeneia has left to summon her maid-servants, Orestes enters with Pylades. It is unusual, though not completely without parallel, for an important character on his first entrance to utter a single line and then plunge into stichomythy. The effect here, of course, is one of haste and furtiveness as the two friends ascertain that this is indeed the temple from which Orestes has been ordered to steal the statue of Artemis. The signs of human sacrifice identify it, and it is a nice touch that the bloodstains on the altar are described as "gold hair," like that of the pillar in the dream (73; compare 51 f). We are reminded that the dream, though wrongly interpreted, has truth in it, but not, as the play will show, the whole truth. And now again, as Orestes tells his story in a protesting apostrophe to Apollo, the lines both grammatically and rhythmically echo the voice of a man distracted. His long opening sentence begins as a question but is left incomplete; as he rehearses his crime and his suffering, he refers to himself alternately in the singular and the plural (78–81), and the line in which he mentions the murder of his mother and his pursuit by "successions of Furies" has metrical substitutions that are astonishing even for Euripides (79). The tone becomes quieter as he narrates how Apollo ordered him to procure the statue that had fallen from heaven onto this remote and barbarous land; but as he surveys the temple and the problem of getting into it (reading ἐμβησόμεσθα at 98), he turns to Pylades in desperation and his speech again becomes disjointed and broken up into a series of short, enjambed questions, one of which is left without a verb. His conclusion is to give up and flee. Orestes' madness and horror are no less vocally transmitted than was Iphigeneia's tender sorrow. Pylades speaks in no such fashion when, in reply, he calms and encourages his friend, but in the level, deliberate manner that characterizes him throughout. It is often hard to attach Euripides' metrical and rhythmical freedom to any point of particular significance, but in this play he seems to have used it as a method of characterization. The characters in the *Iphigeneia* do not possess great depth, but they are very firmly and consistently drawn. Orestes' narrative has introduced one of the chief structural principles of the drama. Apollo, he says, had commanded him to get possession of the statue "by devices or some stroke of luck" (τέχναισιν ἢ τύχῃ τινί). As usual, the oracular command leaves much for the recipient to think out for himself. Here the doubt is cast in terms of the antinomy between τέχνη and τύχη (hereafter techne and tyche), plan versus the unplannable, an antinomy which formed an important part of late fifth century thinking. It is highly prevalent in the romances, one meets with it in Agathon (*Fg.* 6 Snell), and it is basic to the work of Thucydides. In an era when old religious values, or at least religious credence, were under shrewdly questioning scrutiny by the thinkers of the enlightenment, it is not surprising that the feeling should arise that the shape of experience was determined by a combination of human contrivance and uncontrollable chance. Tyche, of course, does not always mean "chance"; it can also be "that which actually occurred," "the event," and this is the more usual meaning in the earlier tragedians. Euripides uses it in both senses (new sense, 501; old sense, 511), but more often to denote the unforeseeable happenings of life, and this was the meaning that was destined to prevail eventually and become deified as the goddess Tyche, Fortune, in the Hellenistic age. The two meanings are not, however, sharply distinct: they simply represent two ways of looking at an event, as a result of a cause, or causes, perhaps understandable only after it has occurred, or as a random by-product of an essentially irrational world never to be understood. It is characteristic of Euripides that he often leaves it open to question as to which view he is taking.

The other term, techne, apart from its meanings of "art," "science," or any skill, can be synonymous (112) with μηχανή (mechane), "plot," "device," "intrigue," and it is by the use of this and/or tyche that Apollo expects Orestes to achieve his end; as Gunther Zuntz puts it, "effort and luck." The third determining element, divinity, will be more fully discussed later. However obscure and of little help the gods of Euripides may be, they are always involved and indispensable to the total dramatic scheme. But first comes the human effort. When Pylades has restored Orestes' courage, he offers a plan: they should hide until night and then try to enter the temple. This structure, though in the distant Crimea, is conveniently built in Doric architecture, and Pylades points to an empty space between the triglyphs where they can climb through. Orestes agrees, remarking:

> It will not be the god's fault if his oracle
> Falls unfulfilled. We must dare the attempt.
> (120–121)

If the god's will is to be done, man must do it. And so the first plan, mechane, is laid; it is now the turn of Tyche, and at first she seems hostile.

The parodos is a kommos, a form that grew increasingly fashionable in later drama. Alternately, Iphigeneia and the chorus of captive Greek girls mourn for the misfortunes of the Pelopid house and their own exile from Greece. The theme of music is touched on lightly as Iphigeneia sings of her "lyreless elegies" (146), and the chorus replies in Asiatic strain, invoking "the Muse that is sung in dirges for the dead." In a later ode, these laments will be replaced by the music of exultation as

the chorus pictures Orestes' ship speeding home triumphantly to Argos (1123 ff). A similar dramatic shift
in the mode of music recurs in the *Helen* where, however, it acquires even deeper significance. During the
song, Iphigeneia performs funeral libations in absentia
for her brother, but her use of the verb "to sprinkle,"
instead of "pour," oddly recalls the presacrificial rites
she described in her dream (161; compare 54). The irony
of holding a funeral service for one who is not dead is
thus delicately compounded with the irony of Iphigeneia's near-fulfillment of her dream. Possibly a kindred irony may be seen in the closing lines, as she sings,

> I wail for my brother
> Whom I left a nursling,
> Still a baby, still young, still a tender shoot
> In his mother's arms and at her breast
> In Argos, sceptered Orestes.
>
> (230–235; compare 834 ff)

"Sceptered" is a startling epithet for a suckling baby, but
it follows well on other contradictions in the play, as
well as confirming Orestes as the lawful heir to both the
glories and the woes of the house of Atreus.

Iphigeneia also tells, for the second time and now in
moving lyrics, the story of her betrayal and "sacrifice"
at Aulis; she feels that there was a curse on her life, not
merely from birth, but from the moment of conception,
a feeling that, again, will be echoed in the *Helen* (213–
216):

> From the very beginning
> An evil daemon was mine,
> From the very beginning, the fatal goddesses
> Of childbed thrust a harsh youth on me,
> Me, courted by all the Greeks,
> First-born branch of the marriage chamber,
> Born of Leda's hapless daughter,
> Slaughter and sacrifice, to her father's shame,

Born to no joy, nursed in prayer for a votive offering.
And they brought me in horses and chariots,
And set me a bride on the sands of Aulis,
Bride, no bride, for Achilles.
                              Ah,
Exiled now, I dwell in the grassless
Realms of the unbefriending sea,
Marriageless, childless, cityless, friendless,
Not singing and dancing for Hera of Argos,
Nor with shuttle before the melodious loom
Weaving pictures of Athenian Pallas
Subduing Titans; but here, at these altars,
Spattering a discord of blood and ruin
Of wanderers, pitiably crying aloud,
Pitiably weeping.
                (203–228; compare *Ion* 196 f, 209 ff)

Naturally enough, the horror of her experience at Aulis
has never left her mind, and her longing for Greece is
mingled with hatred for those who deceived her so bru-
tally and were perfectly willing, for their own ends, "for
Helen's sake" (8), to see her throat cut. She repeatedly
stresses the unnatural cruelty of her father (8, 211, 364 ff,
553, reading κτανών), and her hatred for Calchas, Odysseus, and Achilles is explicit (531 ff). But the situation
is now reversed: the victim of human sacrifice is now the
priestess who commits it, or at least presides over it, and
the Taurians have the impression that she enjoys taking
vengeance in this way (336 ff; 1181 ff). Probably this aspect of the story rests on the original identity of Iphigeneia with Artemis, but dramatically it exploits not
only the contradictoriness of the goddess, but also the
vicious circularity of the principal given element of the
plot, human sacrifice. Suffering breeds hardness of heart,
as Iphigeneia remarks:

Sufferers, who have themselves fared evilly,
Feel no compassion for the unluckier still.
                              (352–353)

Though apparently she would have liked to have gotten Helen and Menelaus into her power (354 ff; compare 458 ff), Iphigeneia has not enjoyed her task, but has been revolted by it (619 f). But now that Orestes is dead, as she supposes, she intends to steel herself and shed no more compassionate tears for her victims (344 ff). Or so she thinks. Her next victim is to be Orestes, and she is instantly drawn to him (472 ff). Her conflict drives her to yet another rehearsal of the Aulis story (359 ff), a long and touching one, and finally to theological speculation on the nature of Artemis herself:

> I find fault with the goddess' sophistries,
> Who, if some mortal bears the stain of bloodshed,
> Or even of childbirth, or should touch a corpse,
> Drives him from her altars as a thing defiled,
> And yet delights in human sacrifice.
> It is impossible that Leto, consort
> Of Zeus, could breed such brainlessness! It's a lie,
> I think, Tantalus' banquet for the gods,
> How they regaled themselves on a child's flesh;
> And these men here, being murderers themselves,
> Foist their own wickedness upon the goddess.
> None of the gods do I consider vile.
>
> (380–391)

This whole speech, with its echo of Pindar's First Olympian Ode—and again, the voice tones are poignantly audible—gives the most concentrated expression to Iphigeneia's dilemma, both personal and religious. To what extent the dilemma was also Euripides' is a question complicated by the dramatic decorum of the character; one should not identify Iphigeneia's youthful reflections too easily with those of the aging Euripides. What is important is that her conclusion, that Artemis cannot be so wicked as she seems, hints at a resolution of sorts, though she takes no action on the basis of it; instead she proceeds with the preparations for the sacrifice. Yet her remark about the Taurians' foisting their own bar-

barities on the goddess foreshadows, with admirable dramaturgical subtlety, the denouement, when the statue is stolen and carried to Attica and a more reputable cult.

One other point must be raised here about Iphigeneia's relation to human sacrifice. It has been asked whether or not she has ever yet sacrificed any Greeks, for there are some apparently contradictory statements about this in the text. In the interchange between Iphigeneia and the cowherd, before the latter reports the capture of the two heroes, Iphigeneia is made to say:

> They have been long in coming; never yet
> Has the goddess' altar reddened with Greek blood.
>
> (258–259)

This seems like a clear enough statement, but one is left to deal with the strong implications to the contrary in 38 f, bracketed by Murray, which states that the law is, and was, to sacrifice Greeks (72), and in 344–347, where Iphigeneia recalls her "tears of kinship" for Greeks who have formerly fallen into her hands. True, at lines 53 and 206, her victims are referred to simply as "strangers," xenoi, but upon hearing that two young men have been captured, Iphigeneia's first question is, "Where are they from?" The answer is, "They are Greeks" (246 f). And finally, the captive who wrote the letter for her must have known Greek, and probably was one. On balance, it seems hard to escape the conclusion that Iphigeneia, to her sorrow, has sacrificed Greeks, or rather, prepared them for sacrifice, for others do the actual slaughter (see 40 f, 621 ff). In fact, it is of some importance that Iphigeneia should have a share in the blood pollution of all the Pelopids, so that she too may be purified in the end. In that case, lines 258–259, quoted above, cannot be genuine, but an interpolation, probably inserted for the same reasons that Murray supported them, to exonerate

Iphigeneia from shedding Greek blood. They are preceded by Iphigeneia's τοῦτο γὰρ μαθεῖν θέλω ("this I wish to learn"), one of several regular tragic formulas that practically require a change of speaker (see 493), and if they are omitted the cowherd's report follows naturally, with its full, expected account of Orestes' madness, Pylades' loyalty, and the rather amusing naiveté of their Taurian captors.

The first stasimon nicely bridges the scenes that precede and follow it. The chorus' opening speculations about who these strangers are, and why they have braved the dangers of the Symplegades and Salmydessus to come to this hostile land, foreshadow the recognition scene to come, while their prayer for Helen's death, pictured with some relish, echoes Iphigeneia's words in her preceding speech (438 ff; compare 354 ff). In fact, the whole final stanza, combining this vengeful prayer with the yearning to be rescued and brought home, reflects, in a way, the heroine's feelings as earlier expressed: the hatred of the land of the Taurians, the longing for Greece, and the thirst for revenge. And throughout it all fine images of the ship itself appear, as she runs her perilous course with her oars foaming and her steering paddles whispering at the stern. Euripides was singularly good at writing about ships and seems to show a strong aesthetic love for them, never missing an opportunity to image their general grace and to describe, in technical terms, the details of their oars, rigging, and tackle. At risk of falling into biographical criticism, one is tempted to reflect that the seaside cave that he used for a study, if the story be true, provided an excellent vantage point from which to observe Athenian shipping, and perhaps inspired this aspect of his work. (See Satyrus, *Vita*, in A. Nauck, *Eur. Trag.* I, vi, 61 ff.)

No two dramas could be less like each other than

Sophocles' *Electra* and the *Iphigeneia*, but there is a situational resemblance that makes it scarcely possible for Euripides to have written his play without recalling Sophocles'. In both, Orestes is reputedly dead, and in both his reunion with a sister brings about salvation. The power of Sophocles' reunion scene lies in the violent shift of emotional tone; never has total despair been more eloquently expressed than in Electra's lament with the urn, and the sudden lift into the heights of rapture comes with the force of an unmodulated shift of key in music, from a somber tonality to a bright, lofty major; for example, the entrance of Donna Anna and Don Ottavio in the Unmasking sextet of *Don Giovanni*. In Euripides the emotional air is by no means so heavily charged; Orestes is calm and resigned to his fate, while Iphigeneia, though pitying her victim, is elated by the knowledge that her brother is alive and may yet save her. But with Sophocles' *Electra* produced, probably, only a short while earlier, Euripides might have felt a challenge, and he answered it by exploiting every dramatic contrivance at his command. The result is the great recognition scene that Aristotle so rightly admired, the longest and most elaborate such scene in all extant tragedy. But it is more than a tour de force; it brings together all, or almost all, the major themes of the play, and by reversing certain statements made earlier by both principals, it becomes a verbal as well as dramatic peripety.

The recognition scene unfolds in four major phases: the questioning (467–577); Iphigeneia's plan (578–642); the debate between Orestes and Pylades (658–724); the recognition proper, preceded by oaths and confirmed by tokens (725–826). Between parts two and three comes a very brief kommos, too brief to interrupt the unity of the whole, and at the end, the conventional recognition duet which, if counted as part of the scene, brings the total to 433 lines, more than twice as long as Sophocles' scene in the *Electra*, and a masterpiece of revelation of character as well as of dramatic suspension. Iphigeneia begins the scene strictly in the role of priestess to Artemis, looking after the preliminary formalities:

> First I must think how all may be in order
> With the goddess' rites. Release the strangers' hands,
> Since being sacred they must not be chained.
> You, go inside the temple and prepare
> What need and custom bid for the occasion.
>
> (467–471)

Animals destined to be sacrificed to a god were ἄφετοι, allowed to roam at will; transferred to a rite of human sacrifice this observance assumes a grim irony, especially since the prisoners are not free to roam, but remain closely guarded, even without chains (638). One sees here an act of purification attending an act of sanctified violence, and recalls Iphigeneia's dilemma about the pure Artemis who cannot look on death, yet demands manslaughter. Iphigeneia's function consists of purifying her victims before they are killed, and, as she explains, she does this by aspersion of holy water; the word is χέρνιψ, normally water used for purifying one's own hands before making sacrifice. Euripides seems to be contrasting such mere ritual purification with the real purification that will result from the action of the play; but the irony is that the result is to be brought about, as Iphigeneia says (1031), by means of the miasma incurred by Orestes when he murdered his mother. Once again there is a kind of vicious circularity, only, as will appear, a new principle will have supervened to make escape possible.

Having begun the ritual, Iphigeneia turns to the captives and, in a wave of pity and instinctive love, begins to question them. Again, there is a complete change of tone as, thinking of her own supposedly dead brother, she cries:

> And your sister, if by chance you have one,
> Of what a pair of youths will she be left
> Brotherless!
>
> (473–475)

If the irony seems a little heavy, it is saved by the emotional voice-quality, rising from the simple devices of prolepsis, exclamation, and the emphatic enjambement of "Brotherless." Throughout the entire stichomythy, the passionate eagerness of Iphigeneia's questions forms a musical contrast with Orestes' dispirited and reluctant answers. The keynote of the scene is tyche, in both of the two senses noted above, tyche as the inscrutable aspect of the world, and as that which actually has happened. She goes on:

> Who knows the event, how and to whom
> Such happenings will come? The gods' affairs
> All move to obscurity, and no one knows
> Evil [or good]. . .
> Fortune suborns all toward the unknowable.
>
> (475–478; for "or good," see Mimnermus, 2, 4–5)

Iphigeneia's sympathy meets with a gloomy deprecation from Orestes, who tells her not to waste her pity since he does not pity himself; and he adds, "One must let one's fortune be" (489). Asked to give his name, he says that it is, or should be, "Unfortunate" (Δυστυχής, 500), thus identifying himself with his fate. But Iphigeneia says, "Give that reply to Tyche," and presses him to tell who he is.

At this point one feels Euripides facing the problem of how to keep brother and sister from recognizing each

other too soon. But he solves it very skillfully; having
first made use of the significant pseudonym, a gambit as
old as the *Odyssey*, he now has recourse to the ancient
belief that to possess a person's name gave one power
over him:

> Or. If I die nameless I may not be mocked.
> Iph. Why do you grudge this? Are you so proud?
> Or. You'll sacrifice my body, not my name.
>
> (502–504)

Orestes' evasiveness is a dramaturgical necessity, but
Euripides has managed to make it plausible, and has
even introduced the antithesis between body and name,
a theme that will be central to the *Helen* (compare *Oed.
Col.* 365 "You fear my name"). Later on he has the same
problem with Iphigeneia, who, upon hearing that Agamemnon is dead, cries out in sorrow.

> Or. Why this lament? Was he your relative?
> Iph. I sorrow for his former happiness.
>
> (550–551)

It is the weakest moment in this otherwise perfectly
constructed recognition scene. Except for the fact that
her feelings about the relationship are equivocal, Iphigeneia has no plausible reason not to say, "Yes, he was
my father"; she must fall back on the old cliché of
mourning for those who fall from bliss to woe. But the
very familiarity of the thought, its sheer expectability,
would probably cause it to pass acceptably before an
audience. Again, when Iphigeneia expresses her hatred
for Helen, it might have been natural for Orestes to
wonder why. Instead, Euripides bears in mind that, up
to the moment of recognition, Orestes is completely absorbed in his own miseries and speaks only grudgingly
of anything else. His ironical reply, therefore, is quite in
character: "I too enjoyed the profits of her marriage"

(526). But it is unnecessary to multiply examples; throughout the questioning, the poet is walking a razor's edge, lest the truth be known before he has deployed the fullness of his invention.

It is significant that, when Iphigeneia asks after the happenings (tychai) in Greece since the fall of Troy, she inquires first about her enemies, Helen, Menelaus, Calchas, Odysseus, Achilles. A certain emphasis thus falls on the strain of vengeful hate that runs through and complicates her native tenderness of spirit. This complication is climactically rendered in a single line when she learns that her father was murdered by her mother; unfortunately there is some doubt about the text, but what she seems to say is: "O miserable, murderess and murderer" (553, reading κτανών). If this reading is correct, it can only be interpreted as showing that Iphigeneia's mourning for her parents is mingled with the unfading memory of her father's willingness to sacrifice her at Aulis. But there is also a structural reason for her to ask about her enemies before inquiring about her own family. Of the latter, she wants to know first about Agamemnon, ambiguously both father and enemy, and when she has heard his fate and her mother's, she goes on to Electra, herself, and last of all, Orestes. The order is a little surprising, in view of her deep devotion to her brother, yet it could be explained on the ground that she thinks him dead; but it is also climactic and points the way to the next phase of the recognition. On hearing that he is alive, Iphigeneia cries joyfully: "False dreams, farewell! You were nothing after all" (589). To which Orestes replies, still brooding on himself and what he feels was his delusion by Apollo:

> Not even the gods, who are reputed wise,
> Are less deceitful than are winged dreams.
> There is much chaos in the ways of gods

As well as men's; one thing alone is clear:
Here is a man who, no fool but persuaded
By mantic words, is lost.

(570–575, following Platnauer)

Orestes extends the falsehood of divination to divinity itself; the world is chaos, a fitting conclusion for a scene whose theme was tyche—fitting at least for Orestes, if not for Iphigeneia.

The news that Orestes is alive sparks off a scene that looks to the future, not to the past; not to what has happened (tyche), but what might be contrived (techne). The plan that Iphigeneia presents cannot properly be called intrigue, for it contains no element of deception, but it is contrivance, mechane. Though her primary aim is her own rescue, yet her design comprises also the rescue of one of the young men, whence her charmingly sententious remark that the best actions are the ones that please everybody (580 f). One of her previous victims, before he died, had been willing to write a letter for her to Orestes, begging him to come and save her, but she had never had anyone to deliver it (588 ff). Presumably the writer of the letter was unable to do so because he had an engrossing engagement with the Tauric Artemis. Some question arises as to how she can save anyone to be her messenger; Platnauer's answer seems best: that she could not spare a lone victim, but that she might spare one of two or more. Such customs were not unknown, as is shown by Herodotus' story of Intaphernes (Hdt. III, 119) and by the reprieve of Barabbas in Matthew (27: 15 ff). In any case, Iphigeneia is fairly convinced that she can persuade the King to release one (742), and she offers freedom to Orestes if he will deliver the letter. Orestes declines in favor of saving Pylades, which brings Iphigeneia to yet another wave of warmth and admiration for this young man, and the wish that her own brother might be just like him. Again, the irony is a little obvious, but again it is redeemed by the tenderness of tone. "For," she says, "O strangers, I am not brotherless," using the word in the same emphatic position as she had earlier (475). Similar, though perhaps a little more delicate, is the irony a few lines later, when Orestes, having learned the details of his immolation, thinks of Electra:

> Or. How might my sister's hand enshroud my corpse?
> Iph. Unlucky man, whoever you are, you pray
>   In vain; she dwells far from this barbarian land.

And she then proceeds to promise him that, since he is an Argive, she herself will adorn his tomb, and she describes the identical rites which she had performed for him in the parodos (156 ff).

The second plan of the drama is now laid, and again it is the turn of tyche. But first, after a brief choral passage contrasting the fates of the two young men, comes the next phase of the recognition process, or rather an interlude in it while Iphigeneia is fetching the tablet with the letter. Pylades is dissatisfied with the plan, and we have an ἀγὼν ἀρετῆς (contest in virtue). He fears that if he allows himself to be saved he will be considered a coward, or even as guilty of having murdered Orestes in order to inherit his kingdom along with Electra. His tone is, as regularly, calm, brave, and sensible. Orestes replies with a speech whose genuine moral loftiness is rare in Euripidean characters, and whose tragic intensity, mingled with ardent appeal, sounds ringingly in every line. He begins simply enough with a commonplace, that it is better to suffer one evil than two, which would happen if Pylades stayed and died with him, and then adds another, that a life as wretched as his own is not worth living anyway. But then the language begins to gain elevation, constantly growing warmer, broken at one place by an anacoluthon, which adds to the emotional tone, and culminating in a handsome apostrophe to his friend:

> But you, if saved, get children by my sister,
> Whom I have given you to keep, your wife—
> My name might live, and my ancestral house
> Never without issue be obliterated.
> But go and live; dwell in my father's house.
> And when you come to Greece and Argos, famed
> For horses, by your right hand, I conjure you:
> Raise me a tomb and place memorials on it,
> And let my sister at the tomb bestow
> Her tears and locks. And tell them, by the hand
> Of an Argive woman, I fell sacrificed.
> Do not betray my sister ever, seeing
> Your union desolate as my father's halls.
>
> Farewell; I have found you dearest of my friends,
> O fellow huntsman, and my foster brother,
> Bearer of the many burdens of my woes.
>
> (695–710)

In the drama preceding Euripides, as far as we know, there are few examples of deliberate self-sacrifice; in fact, in the extant plays, one can think only of Antigone. But Euripides was prepossessed by it, sometimes to the extent of bringing it in rather awkwardly, as in the case of Evadne's suttee in the *Suppliants*. This speech of Orestes is a finely motivated expression of human nobility and love, and deeply connected with the resolution of the play's main moral problem, the self-renewing property of cruelty and evil in general, so explicitly stated by Iphigeneia (352 f). Human sacrifice stands for more than a gory, barbarian ritual; on the deeper level it embraces all the inhumanity, or subhumanity, of man to man, extended into a perpetuity of petty, self-seeking retributive acts. We have called it a vicious circle, sanc-

tioned, apparently, and even demanded by the gods, and
it is significant that Orestes, after his beautiful address
to his friend, should turn on Apollo for having doomed
him by trickery, intrigue (τέχνην θέμενος), and recall
the retributive act that made him a part of the circle:

> But Phoebus, prophet that he is, deceived us,
> And plying his craft, drove us as far from Greece
> As possible, shamed by his former auguries.
> I gave my all to him, trusted his words, slew
> My mother, and am in turn myself destroyed.

(711–715)

It is as if he were saying with Amphitryon, "I, though a
mortal, conquer you, a great god, in virtue" (H.F. 342).
By this very act of magnanimity Orestes has broken the
circle and brought about a moral peripety. Human sacrifice has been replaced by, or one might almost say
turned into, self-sacrifice. The speech is, of course, simply a restatement of his former refusal to let Pylades die
for him, but the rhetorical amplification of that refusal
is needed to emphasize its full moral meaning. Pylades
yields without further dispute, not, one feels, because
he is lacking in nobility, but because Orestes' passionate
words have been too compelling to oppose.

Pylades' closing speech, just before the return of Iphigeneia, brings us back to the theme of tyche. Trying to
keep up Orestes' hopes, he remarks that extremes of
misfortune can produce also extreme changes, "when
it so happens" (721 f). But Orestes can see no help in
Apollo's words; what he sees is Iphigeneia coming back
with the letter and giving directions for the sacrifice.
There is little need to dwell on the splendid dramaturgy
of the recognition proper; it is, of course, the peripety
of the plot, as Orestes' speech is the peripety of the moral
situation. But it is worth observing the interplay of
techne and tyche, which, like gears in mesh, propel the

scene to its inevitable conclusion. Iphigeneia has a plan
by which she hopes to be restored to her home and freedom. Unlike her brother, who tends to extremes of despair and hope, trust and disbelief, she lays her plans with
a cool eye to all possibilities, as will appear more fully
in the great intrigue. So, in mistrust lest Pylades forget
about the letter once he is free, she puts him under oath.
Orestes, in concern for his friend, asks her to swear that
she can and will give him safe conduct. Pylades, who
also has a keen eye for contingency, reflects, in his turn,
that the tablet might be lost at sea, in which case, were
he himself to survive, he should be released from his
oath. But Iphigeneia devises a better solution, to tell him
the contents of the tablet, so that he may, in such a case,
deliver it by memory. As Aristotle observed, all this is a
natural way of bringing the revelation about, but it is
also in accordance with the characters themselves and
with the play's general outlook, that life proceeds by
contrivings and chance happenings, a devious and dan-
gerous path. And so the truth, dexterously withheld by
the poet over hundreds of lines, comes out with elec-
trifying beauty as Iphigeneia recites:

> Say to Orestes, son of Agamemnon,
> She who was slain in Aulis sends these words,
> Iphigeneia, living, whom they think dead.
>
> (769–771)

Orestes' instant reaction, "Where is she? Has she come
back from the dead?" leads first to a mild reproof from
Iphigeneia for interrupting, and then to a bemused interchange between the two young men (we may pass over
the much-disputed order of the lines at this point).
Pylades hands the letter to Orestes, claiming to have fulfilled his vow; Orestes tries to embrace his sister, but is
met by a sharper reproof for defiling a priestess with his
touch. But with the questioning, the truth begins to

emerge. When challenged to give evidence for his claim
to being her brother, Orestes produces tokens that are
rather interesting. He mentions two pieces of weaving
done by Iphigeneia as a young girl. The first represented
the strife between Atreus and Thyestes over the golden
ram, possession of which ensured the kingship; the second showed the sun turning backwards in his course,
the portent by which Zeus confirmed Atreus on the
throne. These two stories from Pelopid history had been
referred to earlier, in a conflated version, by the chorus
(192 ff) as the beginnings of the long series of disasters
that have fallen upon the house. Orestes then asks if
she remembers the sacral water for the wedding bath
sent by her mother to Aulis, and the lock of hair that
she had given her mother at departure. This brings us to
Iphigeneia's own disaster, as well as the juxtaposition of
a purity symbol, the sacral bath, with an act of violence,
the human sacrifice. The last token is the most interesting of all: Orestes says that he has seen the ancient
spear with which Pelops slew Oenomaus and won Hip-
podameia. But Pelops won by cheating and thus brought
down the original curse on the family. The tokens col-
lectively epitomize the crimes and sufferings of the family. But the spear also betokens heroism and suggests
the grander side of Orestes' heritage. He says he saw it
hidden away in Iphigeneia's personal chamber; why this
venerable relic should have been kept there can only be
guessed; perhaps because a token must be privy, which
the spear would not have been had it been on display in
one of the public rooms where any visitor might see it.
Euripides may have intended no more than this by
putting it in Iphigeneia's bedroom; but also he might
have wanted to connect her, as well as Orestes, with the
heroic aspect of the Pelopids, for the plan that she will
soon be devising requires courage as well as guile. The

tokens are not mere superficial, factual evidence; they identify both brother and sister as heirs and products of a criminal, heroic line, and fix their places in it. The symbolism of tokens in the *Ion* reflects even more profoundly, as we shall see, the totality of the drama and its characters.

Through the prevailing joy of the duet that follows the recognition, the dark notes of the Pelopid fatalities are still heard, leading on to a renewed need for salvation, and a new plan. The recovery of her brother brings Iphigeneia to a complete reversal of her former feeling, that she was cursed from the moment of conception; she cries:

> O Cyclopean hearth, O fatherland,
> Beloved Mycenae,
> I give thanks for my life,
> I give thanks for my nurturing.
>
> (845–847)

But presently she is once more rehearsing, for the fourth time, the scene at Aulis, which she refers to again with the word χέρνιψ, suggesting purification, and then moves on in horror to the thought that she had nearly done the same thing to Orestes. Her thoughts are now all for his safety. Her last twenty lines express her agitation in a dizzying assortment of meters as she turns to various possibilities for his escape, only at the very end including her own. She too, like her brother, is finding the spirit of self-sacrifice, which she will openly state in the next episode (1002 ff). Just before the end of her song she invokes three possible sources of salvation: "What god or mortal or unexpected event might show us a way?" (895–899). The last, of course, corresponds to tyche, the "mortal" to human devising, or techne; as for the gods, they have not as yet proved very helpful, but they must be assumed to play some part. Iphigeneia has put very succinctly the motivational triad of the romances.

Orestes expresses it at greater length in his first speech in the next episode. Recalled by the steady Pylades to the necessity for action, and reminded that wise men seize the occasion, "unless they have stepped out of the realm of chance," Orestes exclaims:

> Well said. But Fortune joins us, I believe,
> In this concern; and if a man is zealous,
> More likely it is divinity prevails.
>
> (909–911)

Aeschylus had said something similar in the *Persians* (742), to the effect that whenever a man starts an action a god somehow takes part in it. The reference there was to Xerxes, whose efforts the gods had ruined, contrary to all expectation. Here the unexpectable element has been separated off as tyche, while divinity is regarded as having some possible beneficence. Orestes' language is vague, nor is it clear whether by "divinity" he means Apollo or Fortune. It is hard in fact in this passage to distinguish between divinity and fortune, but they seem to be two ways of looking at human experience, as that which happens, and as that which one has been told will happen. Past and future mingle into a confused present, as Orestes begins to realize that Apollo may not have been the total cheat that he denounced him for (711 ff), and that life may still be redeemed. Salvation, as an off chance, suddenly becomes real for Orestes, and from this moment on, his temperament becomes as sanguine as it has hitherto been melancholy. Salvation comes from the same source as destruction, as he says:

> As many of the Furies heeded not the vote
> Drove us forever in unending flight,
> Until I came to Phoebus' holy ground
> Once more, and stretched before his temple, fasting,

I vowed to end my life there, and at once,
Unless he saved me, he who had destroyed.

(970–975)

Salvation is not to be found without destruction;
Apollo's "holy ground" had commanded Orestes to
commit matricide, and then to find release and purification in the Taurian adventure. Despite confusion, despite the ambiguities of the gods, the human guess at
clarity is not worthless. Formerly ready to give up the
whole attempt, Orestes is now confident that action can
achieve something, and he is ready to try one more time
for purity and peace.

He is not, however, the "hero of many devices"; he is
only a blighted, though brave, wanderer, and it is Iphigeneia who must devise the scheme of escape. The reason for this shift of emphasis is not that Euripides
believed in the essential craftiness of women, despite
the casual line 1032 and similar remarks elsewhere, but
simply because Orestes has never in the play been a man
of techne. It was Pylades who conceived the first plan to
steal the statue, and Iphigeneia who conceived the idea
of sending a message to her brother. Orestes is the victim
of tyche, and as volatile as the goddess herself, either all
hope or all fear. One might have looked to him for a
substantial strategy at this point, given the miraculous
recovery of his sister and renewed hope in Apollo. Instead, he thinks only impractically of killing the King,
and his thoughts are promptly superseded by those of
Iphigeneia. But such helplessness is basic to the character of one who can act, but does not know how to.
And hence the long rhesis (939 ff), where he recounts
his sufferings before and after the trial on the Areop-
agus. From the point of view of Pylades' urgency, this
long, aetiological tale seems contradictory to the concerns of the hour. The speech in itself is interesting, not

only for certain details about the origins of the Areop-
agus court and customary observations at the Anthe-
steria, but also for the form of the myth here adopted.
In the *Eumenides,* Orestes' acquittal at Athens had been
final, and Aeschylus makes no mention of the mission
to the Taurians. Euripides had to blend this wholly different, and doubtless independent, account of the purification of Orestes with the Aeschylean version, which
he could scarcely ignore. He does this by skillfully picking up the equally divided vote of the jurors from
Aeschylus, and applying it to the Furies themselves, so
that some accept the verdict and others do not, thus
leaving Orestes formally acquitted, yet still pursued. But
the real importance of the *rhesis* is that it gives an extended picture of Orestes, whose desperate search for
freedom, like Iphigeneia's, symbolizes the quest after
long-promised, long-delayed salvation, found only in
distant, unlikely lands of the barbarians.

Orestes ends his speech with an appeal to Iphigeneia
to save him, counterpointing her appeal to him in the
letter. Her reply, in turn, counterpoints his earlier decla-
ration of willing self-sacrifice: she will try, if possible, to
save him and herself, but failing that, to save him at
least and die herself (1002 ff). Orestes assures her, however, that their fates are one and that he will not be
saved at her expense, thus rounding off the moral
peripety described earlier. But there is also something of
a theological peripety. Iphigeneia had expressed some
scruples about stealing the holy image of Artemis (995 f),
to which Orestes, his confidence in Apollo now steadily mounting, replies that if such an act were offensive
to the goddess, Apollo would never have ordered it, and
he concludes, on the strength of what has happened so
far, that their hopes of a safe return are good. In a sense,
Artemis too must be saved and transported, as Iphi-

geneia says later, "to a pure house" (1231). All must be purified, Orestes of his madness, Iphigeneia of her involvement in human sacrifice, and Artemis of a cult unworthy of a Hellenic deity. The mystifying interplay of divine and human action is beginning to fall into focus; there is in fact a parallel expressly drawn between the mortal and immortal siblings in Iphigeneia's final prayer to Artemis: "You love your brother, O goddess; consider, I love mine" (1401 f).

This need for genuine purity on all sides is what lends force to the scheme that Iphigeneia now invents, a scheme whose essence is a ritual of purification. Earlier she had spoken of Orestes' crime, in a pointed oxymoron, as a "just evil" (559); now she says that she will put his past horrors to good use by her contrivances σοφίσμασι (1031 ff). Evil is to be turned into good through a pretended ritual of purification which will in fact bring about true purification, even as in the *Helen* misfortune is turned to good account through a pretense at ritual (*Helen* 1082). It is remarkable how little lying Iphigeneia has to do in the hoaxing of King Thoas. We are not, presumably, asked to believe that the statue physically turned on its pedestal, but the gesture is consistent with the nature of a bloodthirsty divinity who cannot look upon pollution. To call Pylades also a matricide is not strictly true, but he was accessory to Orestes' deed. Only two of her statements are outright lies: that the victims had told her that Agamemnon was alive, and that she hates all Greece for its treatment of her (1185 ff). She has explicitly said that she is no longer angry at her father and that she wants to cure her house of its sufferings (991 ff), and it is this new single-mindedness about Greece that has made her ready for, and capable of, salvation. But she must tell these two lies in order to keep Thoas' confidence in her. Everything else is true: she will purify the statue, she will purify Orestes by helping him transport it to Attica, "to a pure house," where she will continue to perform sacrifices, though of a different sort, in its honor. There is no need to labor the irony: the hoaxing scene proceeds briskly, almost gaily, as Iphigeneia dupes the King by telling him what is essentially the truth. There is surely intended humor in the shocked reaction of Thoas on learning that Orestes has killed his mother: "Apollo! Not even a barbarian would have dared that!" (1174). And one feels Iphigeneia warming sweetly to her task when she warns him never to trust a Greek (1205). But the last line that she utters is an affirmation of her faith in the gods "who know more" than mortals. Orestes' gloomy statement about the confused deceitfulness of the gods has found reversal.

Before the intrigue can be put into effect, however, the secrecy and complicity of the chorus must be ensured. Iphigeneia's appeal is another stunning example of poetic imitation of voice tone. Again, the means are simple: pointed enjambement, somewhat loose grammar, parenthesis, and almost breathy repetitions as she turns to one after another of the choristers, begging their help and promising to rescue them if she escapes:

> Keep our secret, and help us to contrive
> Escape. A loyal tongue is good. You see?
> One fate has captured three who love each other—
> Either to return home to our fatherland,
> Or death. If I am saved, you share our fortune,
> I'll save you home to Greece. By your right hand,
> You and you, I beseech you, and you, by your dear
> Cheek, by your knees and all most loved at home,
> Mother and father, and for some, children!
> What do you say? Who says she is willing, who not—
> O speak—to do this? If you rebuff my words,
> I and my hapless brother are both lost.   (1063–1074)

The chorus is won over, and they not only keep the secret but also contribute some delaying tactics later on (1293 ff), thus courting danger for themselves and joining in the spirit of self-sacrifice. For the moment, though, their thoughts are all of home, and in a beautiful ode (1089 ff) they lament their captivity, comparing their dirges to those of the halcyon, always bewailing her husband lost at sea. The first two stanzas contrast the graceful cult of the Delian Artemis with the bloody one of the Taurians, and the third envisions the transference of the goddess to Attica, under the escort of Pan and Apollo, whose celebrant music contrasts with the chorus' own dirges. Euripides cannot resist describing the Argive ship itself, with her fifty foaming oar blades, her sail and forestays flying in the wind over the prow. The last stanza is less closely linked to the action of the play; it returns to the theme of nostalgia, again with a bird image, and ends with a prayer for homecoming, as the choristers recall their girlhood, and how they danced and competed with each other for the most beautiful hair. It is hard sometimes to see how Euripides ever gained the reputation of being a misogynist. He has pictured these girls so winningly that we care about them more than about most tragic choruses (cf. their moving questions, 576 f), and we are glad when they are freed at Athena's command (1467 ff).

The third stasimon, coming directly after the hoaxing scene, takes up for the last time one of the main problems of the play, the relation between divination and divinity. It tells of the birth of Apollo and Artemis, and how Leto carried her infant son to Parnassus where he promptly slew the Python and expelled Themis from the oracular site. In revenge for her daughter's displacement, Earth gives birth to the "nocturnal phantasms of dreams," by which mortals are able to divine past, present, and future, and have no need to honor Apollo's prophecies. But Apollo appeals to Zeus who deprives the dreams of their truthfulness and restores the dignity of Delphi. The mood is playful, but the message is clear. The play had begun with Iphigeneia's dream, which turned out to be false, and we are now told how dreams got to be untrustworthy. They are born of the earth and, as we shall see in the case of the *Ion,* earthborn things carry sinister overtones for Euripides. Throughout most of the play Orestes had been in gloomy doubt about Apollo's motives and truthfulness, and this doubt is reflected lyrically in the momentary eclipse of Delphi by the dreams. But Apollo wins his honor back and Orestes wins his freedom. The dark interims of misapprehension and confusion are cleared at last, by decisive if somewhat unexpected action. The process of the play and the poem is the same, only the poem views it through the eyes of divinity, not suffering humanity; and hence the playful spirit. In the Homeric *Hymn to Apollo* the young god matures with great speed, but he is something more than a baby when he kills the Python. Euripides has chosen the myth of the miraculous infant, a widespread one of which perhaps the most familiar example is Heracles with the serpents. More specifically he seems to have modeled his ode on the *Hymn to Hermes,* where the one-day-old prodigy steals Apollo's cattle and is dragged by his enraged brother before Zeus for justice. Both episodes end with Zeus laughing, in the *Hymn* at Hermes' precocity in the art of lying, here at the infant Apollo shaking his tiny fist in the face of the ruler of the universe. In both also, the honor of Delphi is restored, and a newborn god wins his place on Olympus. The poem is a high-hearted scherzo, a παίγνιον, appropriate to the triumph that is even now taking place.

The exodos calls for little comment, except to note that the messenger's speech gives Euripides another singularly fine opportunity to display his virtuosity in describing a ship in detail: oars, rowlocks, tholepins, rudderslips, catheads, boathooks, the sail blown backwards by a sudden head wind. It is interesting too to note that the adverse heavy seas that drive the ship toward the rocks are due to Poseidon's wrath against the Greeks for their destruction of Troy (1414 ff). This is a tradition that Euripides followed in the prologue of the *Troades*, and there are traces of it even in the *Iliad* (XX, 288 ff), where Poseidon otherwise favors the Greeks strongly. Euripides' use of it in the *Troades* is clearly organic to the dramatic meaning. Here, especially since Orestes had nothing to do with the fall of Troy, it may seem a little arbitrary; but it adds one more touch of mortal danger to the desperate efforts that are the price of redemption, and a further reminder that life proceeds always amid the sway of possibly hostile, as well as favoring, gods. Athena's intervention with Poseidon (1444 f), on the other hand, keeps the balance even. She is, after all, a goddess associated with victory, as well as with the valor and intellect which were necessary components of Iphigeneia's scheme for escape. She validates Iphigeneia's effort more than she effects it; but her motive, to rescue the image of her sister, Artemis, poses a question. Athena is not usually much concerned with Artemis, not, at least, this late in Greek religion, though both were probably, in origin, fertility goddesses. But Athena's prime Athenian epithet, παρθένος, "Virgin," also regularly used of Artemis and often of Iphigeneia, leads the hearer back to the motif of purity, of singleness amid contradictions, born in gods and hard-won by mortals.

For Euripides, as for most Greek poets, the gods are

ambiguous; like the Ghost in *Hamlet,* they seem helpless of themselves, but in the end controlling; which is
to say, they seem to be capable of initiating an action or
situation, but incapable of resolving it without the
human effort which they impose on the characters
involved. The whole tradition about Athena shows her
enmeshed in violence as well as in her virginal inviolability. It is proper that she rounds off the story with the
establishment of the rites at Halae, where the cult of
Artemis Tauropolos will be celebrated, not, indeed, by
human sacrifice, but by the token drop of blood from a
man's neck, lest the cost of purity ever be forgotten. The
transformation of Artemis of the Taurians into Artemis
Tauropolos brings into unity the contradictory aspects
of the goddess, without losing sight of them. But
Euripides is not simply reaffirming an old-fashioned
faith in Hellenic versus barbarian religious practices;
Artemis is "purified," but only by human struggle, and
we are never to forget the expense of blood and tears.
The poet, at the end, is trying to see it from the gods'
point of view—no easy task, since in his day no one
knew who the gods were. Athena's prescriptions for the
ceremonies at Halae prefigure, in part, the intellectual
antiquarianism of the Hellenistic age whose climax was
Callimachus; yet they also suggest something of the
intuition of unchanging truth which is found in
Aeschylus' treatment of aitia, or "origins." The drop of
blood, and the clothes dedicated by women who die in
childbirth summarize not only the paradoxical conflicts
in Artemis, but the necessity of suffering, the pathos of
the lonely, sacrificial gift of love, and the fierce unpre-
dictability of gods who are gradually turning into
chance.

The *Iphigeneia* is the most hopeful of the three
so-called romances. Toward the end, on the simple level

of action, it turns into a tense, confident melodrama; but though the structure and the action necessitate the melodramatic close, more solemn tones are always present, constantly reverberating through the plot, and keeping it in tune with Euripides' lifelong concern for the meaning of divinity as it enters the human scheme. The solemnity centers upon the imagery of sanctity, or purification, oddly joined with some act of violence, whether it be matricide under Delphic command, or Iphigeneia circling the hair of her human victims with lustral water. The theme is constant; it is perhaps most simply expressed by Orestes, in his great speech:

> Tell them, by the hand
> Of an Argive woman, I fell, sanctified
> for slaughter (ἀγνισθεὶς φόνῳ).

The verb means either "to sacrifice," or "to sanctify." It is as if Euripides were considering the ambiguities of the word and emerging with the conviction that all its meanings were bound to necessary, unlovely facts, but all of them additions of the state of humanity.

2

Helen

There has been little agreement among those who have written about the *Helen* as to the category of dramatic composition to which it belongs. Although commonly classed as one of the "tragi-comedies," it has been called everything from a "parody of the *Iphigeneia in Tauris*," a "farce," "no tragedy," and "comedy from beginning to end" to "a brilliant failure," "a powerful and moving drama," "a comedy of ideas," "tragedy *manquée*," and a mixture of "theology and irony." In a situation as desperate as this it is perhaps safest to call it what the Greeks called it, a tragedy, while admitting that it is made up of elements some of which seem ill at ease in the art created by Aeschylus and Sophocles. The situation as a whole, certain tongue-in-cheek utterances, and above all, perhaps, the character of Menelaus undoubtedly suggest that Euripides was not being very serious. But if that were the whole truth, it would be hard to account for the divergent variety of the labels just listed. For the play also comprises genuine tragic suffering and what seems to be perfectly serious philosophy; so that the designation "Theology and Irony," which is that of Gunther Zuntz, seems to come closest to Euripides' intentions. Indeed, Zuntz's essay and the one by Anne Pippin Burnett both contain excellent insights, especially in that they recognize Euripides' complex, dissonantal mingling of conflicting points of view, which is observable in all his works, and not least in this one. No poet ever had a greater gift for seeing everything in two ways at once; the question is, can criticism resolve the dissonance without spoiling its effect or destroying it?

To call the *Helen* a play about truth and seeming may not be very helpful, for all drama is after a fashion about truth and seeming. But the *Helen* is more explicitly so than most, because of the nature of the myth itself. The story of Helen in Egypt existed in several forms in antiquity. The *Odyssey* (IV, 351 ff) brings her there with Menelaus after the fall of Troy. Herodotus (II, 113 ff) tells how Paris, after escaping with her, is driven off his course to Egypt where King Proteus summarily interns her for safe keeping and sends Paris home. The Greeks take Troy but find no Helen, who is finally reunited with Menelaus when he is driven by storms to Egypt. But the most famous version was that of Stesichorus of Himera, who was said to have been blinded by the deified Helen for having condemned her elopement with Paris. In order to regain his eyesight he composed a palinode, or rather two, one each against Homer and Hesiod, reversing the traditional tale and declaring that Helen never went to Troy, but that what Paris carried off was a phantom Helen, while she herself was spirited away to Egypt (Stes. *Fgs.* 15, 16 Page). Menelaus recovered her in perfect chastity, and Stesichorus recovered his eyesight. How much of all this is the poet's invention is not known; there may have been a Spartan myth to this effect (see Eur. *Electra* 1278 ff). Spiriting-away is a very common motif in both epic and folklore (for example *Iliad* V, 449) and the substitution of a phantom for the object of desire finds a parallel in the story, as told by Pindar in *Pythian* II, of Ixion, who made an attempt on Hera but was fooled by Zeus into sleeping with a cloud in her shape, and was then damned to eternal torments. Whoever invented the phantom Helen, or *eidolon*, Euripides' choice of this version set the main theme of the play, and the kindred antinomies, body *versus* name, reality *versus* appearance, occur constantly throughout, pointing to the elusiveness of truth amid ironical webs of ignorance. It has been ably shown that the formal contrast between name and body originates in the late plays of Euripides, and that he was probably influenced by the cognition theories of Gorgias, and thus led to the problem of the difficulty, not to say impossibility of true knowledge. The theme is sounded right at the start when Helen casts doubt on the account of her own birth from an egg engendered by Zeus:

> Sparta my fatherland is far renowned,
> My father Tyndareus. But there is a tale
> How Zeus, taking the likeness of a swan
> Fleeing an eagle's onslaught, winged his way
> To Leda, my mother, and so won deceitful
> Wedlock with her, if the tale is true.
>
> (16–21; compare 256 ff)

But the birth of Helen from an egg is only one in the series of implausibilities which distinguish the *Helen*. Whereas in the *Iphigeneia in Tauris* Euripides took pains that an almost identical plot should not put too great a strain on the credulity of his audience, in the *Helen* he seems to seek the implausible deliberately and to underscore the unlikelihoods of his tale. The result is that, for all their similarity, there is a great difference between the two plays, the *Iphigeneia* being more properly called melodrama, while in the *Helen* the emphasis on the improbable, the magical, the unascertainable suggests rather the term romance. The terms perhaps do not matter, but the difference does, for the romantic mode admits of a far wider play of imagination and requires greater suspension of disbelief, together with more of the element of reflection and a more distanced perspective. Thus perhaps we should not inquire too closely as to how Egypt came to be supplied with a chorus of captive Greek girls (192 f), though in *Iphigeneia* we are given more details about the captivity of the choristers in the Crimea (1106 ff); or how Helen can maintain herself night and day as a suppliant at the altar-tomb of Proteus; or why the superstitious naiveté of Thoas should be inflated into the monumental gullibility of Theoclymenus. All this is part of the exaggerative, dreamlike mode of romance. Euripides appears to have been the first to make dramatic use of that mode, and his source for it is most likely to have been the *Odyssey*, which, as we have seen, had its own version of Helen's sojourn in Egypt. Though Euripides did not adopt that version, yet his play has something of the mysteriousness and provoking quality of Telemachus' visit to Sparta in Book IV. It is as if, while telling a wholly different, indeed opposite story about Helen, he adopted some of the tone of the *Odyssey*.

As the play opens, Helen is sitting at the tomb of Proteus. Her prologue, in typically Euripidean style, sets the scene and gives the antecedent history, beginning with genealogy. Proteus in the *Odyssey* had been a minor sea deity, but by Herodotus' time, if not sooner, he had become a legendary King of Egypt, famed for his uprightness. He had not lost all connection with the sea, however, for he had married a Nereid, Psamathe, formerly the wife of Aeacus, by whom he had a son, Theoclymenus, now the ruler, and a daughter, Theonoe, who inherits her grandfather's truthful clairvoyance and wisdom. Helen then speaks of herself, her dubious birth, and goes on to relate how and why she was spirited away to Egypt. Hera, it seems, angry at her defeat in the beauty contest judged by Paris, contrived her disappearance through the agency of Hermes, and substituted a living *eidolon*, "made out of sky (οὐρανοῦ ... ἄπο), for Paris to carry off (compare *Bacchae* 292 and Dodds *ad loc.*). By this means she hoped to get revenge on Aphrodite by exposing her for a cheat who did not fulfill the marriage she had promised. Now of course Athena, equally a loser in the beauty contest, might have devised the same trick for the same motive, or for the better one of punishing Paris, or, as protectress of heroes, to save Menelaus from harm as she saved him in the *Iliad* from the arrow of Pandarus (IV, 127 ff). But there would have been little point in having Athena act so, and it would have jarred with her traditional character. It was entirely in accord with Hera's traditionally jealous, conniving nature to think up such a plan, but there is a further point as well. Hera is, of course, the patroness of legal marriage, and it is appropriate for her to protect it and to vitiate Aphrodite's irresponsible variety of sex. The antithesis between the two goddesses corresponds exactly to the play's basic antithesis of truth and seeming, or, more concretely, to the ambiguous situation of Helen herself: she is, in fact, the innocent wife of Menelaus, but the world knows her as an adulteress and the cause of a disastrous war. The strife between the two goddesses, which is much like that in the *Hippolytus*, only more subtly handled, reaches its culmination later on, in one of the most mysterious, and disputed, passages in the play (878 ff).

The whole structure of truth and seeming in the *Helen*, as in the *Iphigeneia* and *Ion*, differs from the usual one of earlier tragedy where the revelation of truth brought suffering as a rule, if not inevitably. Here it is seeming that entails suffering—the seeming infidelity of Helen, the seeming death of Menelaus—while the truth, when it comes, brings joy and release. And yet, as will be seen, the release cannot be accomplished or the joy complete without further veils of seeming in the form of intrigue.

As in the *Iphigeneia*, the prologue has two parts, monologue and dialogue, but unlike that of the *Iphigeneia* the two halves bear no particular structural relation to the play as a whole. Indeed, the structure of the *Helen* is its least impressive aspect. Teucer's arrival is rather feebly motivated, and furthermore, why Teucer? He does, indeed, harshly convey to the innocent Helen the Greeks' hatred of her, but apart from the fact that, like Helen, he is suffering an undeserved exile, his connection with the plot is merely that of a messenger; he is given little or no character, certainly less than the unnamed messenger who appears later. Euripides seems to have used him because he was the only Achaean hero whose wanderings led him, on his way to Cyprus, past Egypt where he could answer Helen's questions about Troy. Thematically, however, he is relevant enough. He sets up a new screen of illusion by leading Helen to believe that Menelaus has been lost at sea, and his refusal to believe that the real Helen stands before him foreshadows that of Menelaus later on. Naturally she makes no effort to convince him, since his first impulse had been to shoot her, but she does ask cautiously about what happened to "Helen" when the city was taken:

> *Helen* And did they also seize the Spartan woman?
> *Teuc.* Menelaus drove her forth, dragged by the hair.
> *Helen* You saw the poor woman, or do you speak
>   hearsay?
> *Teuc.* With my own eyes, no less than I see you.

Helen Take care, lest you caught a phantom, made by the
    gods.
Teuc. Think of some other subject; no more of her.
Helen Are you so sure the phantom was the truth?
Teuc. I saw with my own eyes. And the mind sees.

                      (115–122)

Whatever the precise meaning of the final phrase,
apparently a quotation from Epicharmus, it is clear that
Teucer stands firm, and that Helen's intimations have
accomplished no more than a reiteration of the theme
of deceptive experience. In the next few interchanges
Helen, besides hearing of Menelaus' death, learns that
her mother has committed suicide, and that her two
brothers have done the same, according to one story,
and according to another that they have become stars—
a further ambiguity attendant on the main theme.
Teucer has now just about served his purpose and must
be eliminated. Abruptly changing the subject, he tells
why he came, only to learn that he must flee as
fast as possible. He has come to ask the prophetic
Theonoe the way to Cyprus, where he is to found a
colony "named with an island name" (Salamis, 149).
Why he needs Theonoe, since he already has oracles
from Delphi, is not explained, but perhaps we are to
assume that he, like Aeneas, was not sure where his des-
tination lay. Helen's answer, "The voyage itself will
show you" (151) has been adroitly connected by
Murray (*ad loc.*) with a passage in the *Bacchae* (406 ff)
where it appears that there was an ancient belief that
currents originating in the Nile swept eastward to lap
the shores of Cyprus. Teucer, not pausing to investigate,
takes immediate leave on learning that Theoclymenus
kills all the Greeks whom he can find. As he goes, he
pronounces a curse on the phantom Helen whom he has
seen, and a blessing on the real Helen whom he gal-

lantly excuses for looking like her. Perhaps his words serve to foretell the happy outcome, but one feels that Teucer has been somewhat opportunistically exploited and peremptorily dismissed. But be it remembered that he is a person in a prologue, essentially a messenger, and also that the mode of romance is less concerned with individuals as such than with the experiencing of the unexpected in mysterious places.

Helen begins her great lament with what appears to be a deliberate echo of Stesichorus. In his second Palinode Stesichorus had used the phrase "Virgin with golden wings," and Helen invokes the Sirens as "Winged maidens, virgin daughters of Earth" (167 f; Stes. *Fg.* 16, Page). It would be natural for Euripides in any case to echo Stesichorus, but the context here may be of further significance. The *Helen*, like the other two romances, concerns ultimate salvation, and in the Ode on the Great Mother (1301 ff) the idea of "music redeeming life" has been rightly discerned. Stesichorus had redeemed his sight by song, and Helen, using almost his phrase, calls on the Sirens, as singers, to bring her music. It may be fanciful to find here a prayer for redemption, but the idea that music has power to redeem men and actions from oblivion is common in Greek literature, from the myth of Orpheus on. As yet, however, the songs are only laments, and no redemption seems possible, though it is interesting to note that Persephone is also invoked, and elsewhere she is mentioned only in the Great Mother Ode, where her return from death is implied, if not actually described. But here, of course, she is simply Queen of the dead, and the Sirens too, at least in this version, are daughters of Earth, death goddesses, one of whose functions was to mourn for Persephone. It is a deathly music that Helen invokes, but one connoting eventual reprieve.

When the chorus has entered, Helen pours out her sorrows, and the chorus joins in the dirge, so that the parodos again takes the form of a kommos, as in the *Iphigeneia*. Considerable prominence is given to the suffering of the Trojans: it is the first thing that Helen mentions (196 ff), and she closes her final stanza with a reference to it (248 ff). She had expressed sympathy earlier for the Trojans (109), and in a later lyric she bursts into a full lament for them and for the Greeks also (362 ff). Always she seems to feel as guilty as if she had actually done the things she is reputed to have done:

> The ruins of Ilium
> Are given over to hostile flame,
> Because of me, slayer of many,
> Because of my name of many woes.
>
> (196–199; compare 363 ff)

True, she reminds herself that it was only her name, her phantom, that had caused the war, that she herself is innocent; but that fact, as she explains in the *rhesis* that follows, only makes her ill fame harder to bear than if it were grounded in actuality (270 ff). In a sense she is both innocent and guilty, for her beauty did cause the war, even if she was saved from eloping with Paris. It is a kind of empty innocence, for she has done nothing to preserve it, except for resisting the advances of Theoclymenus—a situation that has not as yet come to real dramatic involvement. And so she feels guilt and expresses it in tones that distantly recall those of the Helen of the *Iliad*. She considers herself the murderer of her mother and deserter of her daughter, and "dead in every manner save in fact" (280 ff). Always gifted in the art of ambiguity, Euripides has managed to give his Helen her full load of sensed guilt, while at the same time presenting her in the image of feminine perfection. Adverting again to her birth from an egg, she calls her-

self a τέρας, an ambivalent word connoting both mar-
vel and monstrosity (256 ff following Renehan's text),
and the cause is partly Hera and partly her own beauty.

The notion of beauty as a disaster, either to oneself or
others, is very old: as examples of the latter, besides
Helen, one thinks of Paris (Il. III, 39, 54 f) and Pandora,
whom Hesiod calls a "lovely evil" (Theog. 585).
Sophocles in the Trachiniae represented both Deianeira
and Iole as victims of their own beauty (Tr. 25, 465), and
so too was Iphigeneia (Iph. T. 20 ff). These are casual
references to what appears to have been something of a
commonplace. But the theme in the first part of the
Helen is insistent; Helen brings it up no less than five
times in less than four hundred lines (27, 236 f, 304 f,
261, 375 ff), which suggests that Euripides intended
more than a commonplace. In the other cases beauty
had indeed entailed disaster, but Helen is the archetype
of the idea, and in this play, where she is innocent of
any misdeeds, it becomes the paradoxical essence of her
life, quite consonant with the Euripidean duality in all
things. She is indeed a τέρας, a fatale monstrum, and
she finally felicitates Callisto and Ethemea for being
transformed by Artemis into beasts "because of their
beauty" (383), a kind of climax to the marvel-monster
motif. But no such metamorphosis is in store for her,
and she threatens suicide, both at the end of her rhesis
and in the lyric that follows (298 ff, omitting 299–302;
348 ff).

Between these two passages the chorus has reminded
Helen that Teucer's report of the death of Menelaus may
not be true; she replies that he had clearly declared it
(306 ff). He had not, in fact, but twice called it hearsay
(126, 132). Somewhat as Iphigeneia misinterprets her
dream, Helen believes in the worst without proof: seeming must be maintained as long as possible. But at the

chorus' urging she agrees to consult the all-knowing Theonoe who can tell her the truth; the chorus goes with her, and we wonder why. The few other examples of the chorus' leaving the orchestra are necessitated by a change of scene, but there is nothing of the sort here; instead, the only reason given is the rather feeble cliché that women should help each other (329). Helen does not need their help, but Euripides needs their absence so that Menelaus may enter alone. It would have made impossible the fine scene of his meeting with Helen had the chorus been present to explain the truth to him, as would have been inevitable in the familiar type of scene where a new character enters and exchanges questions and answers with the coryphaeus. The choral exit is a little awkward, structurally, but there is a further reason for it. In a drama that is built around the reunion of two long-lost people, it is, as we have seen in the *Iphigeneia*, a strong dramatic device to use a double prologue, as it might be called, in which the two principals enter separately but do not immediately make contact with each other. Euripides, in his *Electra*, used a modified version of it, appropriately since his play's climax is not the recognition scene. In the *Helen* he modified it still further, for a simple double prologue would have been virtually impossible. Instead, he removed the chorus rather arbitrarily and let Menelaus deliver a second prologue beginning as usual with genealogy and self-identification, and proceeding to an explanation of the circumstances.

Menelaus himself has always been a puzzle. More than any other single feature of the play he has led critics to think of it as a comedy. The long-awaited hero arrives shipwrecked and cursing his fate, boasting, despite his disclaimer (393), of his victory over Troy on the one hand, and mourning on the other at his present helplessness. Above all, he is concerned about his clothes, or rather lack of them; his whole glorious wardrobe has been lost at sea, and he is reduced to garbing himself in salvaged bits of sailcloth and rigging, a source of great embarrassment to him. All in all, he does at first seem like a mere parody of the mighty brought low, and especially when he is verbally and physically abused by the old porteress and reduced to tears. But to conclude this and no more would not be quite supportable. All are agreed that late Euripides had a highly formative effect on the New Comedy; but what is meant is that he introduced a somewhat lighter tone into certain tragedies and developed plots involving long-lost people and intrigue. It does not mean that, after nearly 400 lines of serious tragic poetry, he would tastelessly insert a scene of broad comedy; Euripides often indulges in angular discontinuities, and there are certainly touches of humor in the three romances and elsewhere, but there is no such thing as straight comic "relief," no Porter scene as in *Macbeth*.

There were traditions out of which Euripides made his figure of Menelaus, nor is this the first time he has been shown as a bit ludicrous. On the Attic stage he is regularly represented as a fool, a knave, or at best helpless. In the *Iliad* he is a rather ordinary figure, distinguished in neither of the two accomplishments that define a hero—namely the doing of deeds and speaking of words—but bluff, honest, and brave. In the *Odyssey*, however, he is rather ridiculous. After all his trials (and errors) he has settled down with Helen, a likable, contented cuckold with a head more remarkable for horns than brains. He fails to recognize Telemachus by his resemblance to Odysseus, though Helen does so in a flash. When an omen appears, he ponders it and Helen interprets it (15, 160 ff). Most remarkable of all, he recounts, apparently with naive approbation, how Helen, on the night Troy was taken, came down to the Wooden Horse and there called to the men within, imitating the voice of each one's wife, so that Odysseus had to restrain them from answering, and thus exposing the plot. It is clear that he not only lets his wife do his thinking for him but that also he is completely under her spell, though at first, after Troy fell, he had meant to kill her (*Ilias Parva* XVII [Oxford]; compare Ar. *Lys.* 155 f, and Schol. Eur. *Androm.* 627 ff). Certainly Homer's picture is more subtle than Euripides', as it had to be in the eulogistic mode of epic, but this is not the first time Euripides has cut a hero down to human size.

The fact that there was Homeric precedent for making Menelaus a combination of the valorous and the ludicrous does not in itself save the scene from being, perhaps, inappropriately comic; at most it reduces the surprise by linking such a portrait to tradition. Menelaus was always more or less like that, but Euripides has exaggerated perhaps to a damaging degree. He doubtless intended some humor, but the question is, how much, and did he allow more than he intended? Menelaus starts off seriously enough, recounting his victory over Troy, his subsequent wandering and shipwreck; the tone is somewhat boastful, but scarcely that of a braggart soldier, as has been said. A certain homeliness enters when he comes to his embarrassment about his clothes, a matter to which we shall return. He then calls at the palace gates and receives a rude response. This is indeed a motif frequent in comedy, but there it usually involves terror or horror on one side or the other, or on both. Here there is only the rebuff from the old woman. Menelaus' behavior, as he cringes before her pushes and threats, is, of course, completely unheroic, but he is a suppliant and suppliants need not act heroically. He weeps when he compares his former triumphs with his present plight, but Achilles and Odysseus weep also on occasion. So far he is a little ludicrous, but he is also rather appealing. Much would depend on how the role was acted, for though the scene could possibly be played directly for laughs, that does not seem to be inevitable or in harmony with the poet's total aim. Rather, the character of Menelaus partakes of the Euripidean sense of the duality in all existence, mentioned earlier, and pervasive throughout.

There remain the clothes. There are any number of references to Menelaus' attire, both while he is in rags and after he has been suitably fitted out later on, so that they must be considered thematic. The figure of the reduced king in rags had distinguished forebears in the *Odyssey*, the *Persians* of Aeschylus, and doubtless elsewhere; he appears as well in the very late plays of Sophocles. In Euripides' hands, the staging of tattered royalty had become a kind of mannerist theatricalism that provided Aristophanes, in 425 B.C., with one of the most hilarious scenes in the *Acharnians*. Homely as it may seem as a motif for tragedy, clothing is, among other things, a status symbol, and one used elsewhere as such by Euripides (*El.* 305, *Ion* 239, 326). More important, it has been pointed out that Menelaus' clothes are merely another concrete symbol of the basic theme, appearance versus reality, and that he recovers his true self once he has put on proper clothing. It is perhaps this circumstantial, momentary loss of self that accounts for his overassertiveness about his accomplishments at Troy and the power of his own name to carry weight anywhere in the whole world (501 ff). There is considerable irony in this last remark, coming as it does directly after he has been forced to the conclusion that many people and places may have identical names, and that therefore there is nothing surprising in finding another woman named Helen, daughter of another Zeus and coming from a different Sparta, in the royal palace in Egypt (497 ff). Menelaus' mental processes are droll, but the point is not whether he should, or could, have immediately realized that he had been chasing a phantom for seventeen years; the point is that he is acting out the difficulty of arriving at the truth without realizing that he himself, like everyone, is subject to ambiguity and delusion. Once more, we meet with the Gorgian theories of cognition. The insistent playing on the theme of names suggests a kind of rudimentary nominalism, and it is perhaps not insignificant that the old woman calls Helen the daughter of Zeus and then, two lines later, the daughter of Tyndareus (470, 472). Helen's two patronymics are frequent in Greek literature, but their close juxtaposition here reminds us of her own doubts about her parentage and of the haunting question of identity, which is the burden of the next scene.

If Menelaus' arrival had introduced some touches of humor, Helen's return with the chorus restores a degree of the previous air of seriousness. The recognition process itself is less tense and drawn out than in either *Iphigeneia* or *Ion*, for it is not the climactic scene. Also the form is unusual; Helen, acute and penetrating as she was in the *Odyssey*, recognizes Menelaus easily when she really looks at him, though at first, because of his clothes, she takes him for a wild man (554). But Menelaus refuses to believe what he sees or what Helen tells him. Her tragic desolation deepens before the obtuseness of her longed-for savior. No use is made of tokens. Helen had mentioned them in an earlier, and probably spurious, passage (290 ff), but they would be pointless anyway, since Hera had presumably equipped the *eidolon* with all the knowledge possessed by the real Helen. The problem is to make Menelaus believe what is unbelievable, or at least not dreamed of in his simple philosophy; consequently, the emphasis of the recognition scene falls less on the revelation of fact than on the delusiveness of experience. The irony of Menelaus' taking the real Helen for a phantom, and not a friendly one at that (569), leads to a fuguelike concentration of the thematic words of the play:

> Helen I did not go to Troy; it was a phantom.
> Men.   And who is this that fashions living bodies?
> Helen Aether. Your "wife" is a figment of the gods.
> Men.   And which god fashioned it? Incredible!
> Helen Hera; she made a changeling, to baffle Paris.
> Men.   How could you be here and in Troy as well?
> Helen The name could be many a place, but not the body.
>
> (582–588)

Phantom, Aether, figment, the unbelievable, deceptive exchange, duality, name versus body: one need not be so slow-witted as Menelaus to be confused by it. Actually, part of the effect of the scene on the reader, whether intended or not by the poet, is to raise some doubt about which is the real Helen after all. This is because we see it from Menelaus' point of view, and the story is at least unlikely.

The messenger who brings the truth is more prepared to believe in miracles. He preludes his account by saying that the wonder he is about to relate is not merely one in name, but in fact—a rather gratuitous sounding of the theme—and also that Menelaus' labors have been in vain (601, 603; compare 730). The vanity of the war, implicit throughout, now becomes explicit, making the suffering and guilt of war all the more poignant. In fact, the departing phantom's first words as she rises into the air express pity for the Trojans and the Greeks, in that order, as the real Helen had done. The messenger's reaction at seeing Helen again before him is rather amusing; "I didn't realize that you had wings," he says, accepting another miracle; "but I won't let you mock us again; you've caused your husband and his allies enough trouble" (616 ff). The phantom has disappeared, the truth is revealed, but the messenger's misapprehension marks a final extension of the confusion theme, together with a reminder of the sufferings at Ilium. Indeed the tragedy and vanity of the war pervade the whole first half of the play, appearing in the lyric duet that follows the recognition (691 ff), in the messenger's remarks about the worthlessness of prophets who might have averted the disaster (744 ff), and later as the chief burden of the fine ode at 1107 ff. It has been denied that the *Helen* is an antiwar play, and certainly protest against war is not its primary concern; but the motif is too prevalent to be ignored—not surprisingly, three years after the *Trojan Women* and one year after the defeat in Sicily. It makes it hard to read the play, as some have, as "comedy from beginning to end."

As we have seen, the *Iphigeneia* is built on a wonderfully intricate interweaving of the forces of tyche and techne, chance and intrigue. The two rather divide the *Helen* between them, tyche dominating the first part up to the disappearance of the phantom, and techne the second part. The messenger sums up the former in his speech on the inscrutability of the gods and life itself:

Daughter, how devious and inscrutable
Is god: with ease somehow he twists all things
Bringing them hither and thither. One man toils,
Another, effortless, yet comes to grief
With nothing sure amid unending chance.
You and your husband had your share of pain,
You in repute, and he by war's exertion.
But striving won him nothing; now he has fared
To happiest blessings, come of their own accord.

(711–719)

It is now time to devise a plan of escape, but there are many preliminaries. In a leisurely stichomythy Helen learns to her dismay that Menelaus, in his desperation, has been begging at the palace gates; Menelaus replies "That was the fact, but it didn't have that name," which sounds like another overplaying of the name–fact motif, and a rather meaningless one. The lines (788–792) could be an interpolation, but Euripides is not above such little excesses. Menelaus learns that Helen has taken asylum at the tomb of Proteus because Theoclymenus wants to possess her and kills all Greeks on the chance that one might be Menelaus. The theme of purity, barely mentioned in the prologue (48), now reappears as she assures her husband that she has kept her bed untouched (795). Also the theme of self-sacrifice enters with Helen's urgings that Menelaus flee and leave her behind; and this leads on to the agreement that, if they can find no means of escape, they will die together by the same sword (835 ff). Menelaus confirms this in a speech that, far from being vain heroics, is rather touching:

> I will not shame the glory won at Troy,
> Nor go to Greece and there receive much blame,
> I who bereaved Thetis of Achilles,
> And looked on Telamonian Ajax' blood
> And Nestor childless; shall I not deem it fit
> To die myself for the sake of my own wife?
>
> (845–850)

If Menelaus can boast of his glory won at Troy, he can equally well take the responsibility for the many deaths he caused. There remains, however, the possibility of a device, as Helen has said (813), but the only hope of carrying it out, or even of contriving it, is to persuade the all-knowing Theonoe to conceal Menelaus' arrival from her bloodthirsty brother. Helen had been told by Theonoe that Menelaus was alive and would come in time, but in her joy she had forgotten to ask whether or not he would survive coming (536 ff). This timely forgetfulness, which incidentally recurs in the *Ion*, allows for the mysterious crucial scene to come.

Theonoe is a remarkable creation, quite without parallel among the characters of extant Greek drama. Cassandra comes nearest, but Cassandra is a helpless victim, while Theonoe is in control. Her real name is Eidó, and Euripides probably took it from Eidothea, the sea nymph who helped Menelaus in *Odyssey* IV (compare Aesch. *Fg.* 212 N. = *Fg.* 5 M. from the *Proteus*). But the shorter form is highly suggestive; it connotes three words, all from the same root: εἰδέναι, to know, εἴδομαι, to seem, and εἰδώ, beauty. (Hesychius glosses the common noun εἰδώ as both φρόνησις and ὄψις.) Thus, quite in herself she summarizes the essence of the play, and those who find her central to its interpretation are quite right. An aura of piety and purity surrounds her; her virginity is stressed (10, 894, 939, 1008), and when she enters she is bidding her attendants purify the air with sulphur and flaming torches so that she may "receive the pure breath of heaven" (867). The word that she uses for air is αἰθήρ, aether, which has appeared in numerous contexts before and now will acquire a deeper meaning. Her omniscience includes even the activities of the gods, whence her epithet Theonoe, and it is specifically to announce such activities that she has come.

After pointing out that her prophecy of Menelaus' coming has been fulfilled, Theonoe tells Helen that there will presently be a dispute between Hera and Aphrodite before Zeus and the assembled gods, Hera wishing to see Menelaus come safely home with an innocent wife and thus prove Aphrodite a fraud, Aphrodite striving to prevent that by destroying them. The situation seems a little bizarre, somewhat like a traditional psychostasia, but be it remembered that the struggle between the two goddesses corresponds on the divine level to the struggle between truth and seeming. The irony of it all is that it was not Aphrodite but Hera who committed the fraud, and created the seeming, by creating the *eidolon*, and to represent Aphrodite as a cheat would make only another veil of seeming, though at the same time revealing the truth about Helen's chastity. It is an infinite regress; appearance and reality are inseparable components of the world as it is, the gods included.

Theonoe's next words have been the source of some confusion. They have seemed, in the eyes of most scholars, to imply that it is not Zeus who will decide the case but Theonoe herself. Her words τέλος δ' ἐφ' ἡμῖν have generally been translated "The decision rests with me," that is, whether she will take Aphrodite's side and tell her brother that Menelaus has come, as she is under strict orders to do, or suppress the news and favor Hera. Recently Gunther Zuntz has argued that τέλος δ' ἐφ' ἡμῖν cannot, either grammatically or theologically, mean "The decision rests with me," but simply "Finally, what I must decide is." The τέλος would then have its usual meaning, and form simply the third limb of a μὲν ... δὲ ... δὲ construction. He also contends that it is absurd to suppose that the gods' disputes could be settled by the arbitration of a mortal. Grammatically he is, of course, right: τέλος does not naturally mean "decision," and though it perhaps could be made to, it is doubtful that any Athenian would so understand it, coming as it does in such a common construction. But theologically there is more to be said. The gods are sometimes partly affected, or even controlled by the actions of men. Zeus states openly that he cannot steal the body of Hector from Achilles (*Iliad* XXIV, 71 ff), and, as we shall see, Creusa's actions in the *Ion* upset Apollo's plans; Athena puts the case of Orestes before a human jury, and as for direct human arbitration in divine disputes, one need only recall the Judgment of Paris. One of the distinguishing features of Greek polytheism, down to the philosophic era, is the interplay of divine and human action, most vividly seen in the double motivations in the works of Homer and Sophocles. And so here, if one agrees that the fate of Helen and Menelaus depends on whether or not Theonoe tells her brother, then it follows logically that the verdict of the goddesses' dispute rests with her. The phrase τέλος δ' ἐφ' ἡμῖν does not mean it, but dramatically it is the fact. If Theonoe tells her brother, Hera cannot possibly win; if she does not, she gives the lovers a chance, but they must still pray to Hera not to change her mind (1024 ff). For Theonoe to decide which action she will take is to settle the goddesses' strife. There is, of course, no question of direct intervention by either deity.

It might be asked why, if everything depends on the human level, do the goddesses come in at all at this point? It was suggested above that their quarrel further complicates the inextricable toils of truth and seeming; the gods apparently are not consistently on one side or the other; instead, they perpetuate, sometimes for the meanest reasons, the utter confusion of the world. But the gods have also their grandeur; they are the enlarging mirrors of experience, and to have them involved in the fortunes of Menelaus and Helen adds a new dimension, and a longer perspective on the world's structure and happenings. Theonoe alone has that perspective. But clear-sighted as she is, she is no less involved in the scheme of appearance and reality than the others. If she is to permit the truth about Helen to emerge, she must do it by suppressing a truth, a truth that if told will perpetuate a lie originally devised by a goddess.

It is an interesting, though unanswerable, question whether Theonoe foresees what decision she will make. One thing she does foresee is that if she does not tell Theoclymenus she will suffer for it, and she promptly calls for someone to deliver the news (892 f). This line has unnecessarily bothered scholars on the grounds that she has dismissed her attendants, presumably, at 871 f; but it is by no means clear whether or not they have yet left the stage, and if they have it accounts for her asking, "Who will go and tell?" rather than simply appointing somebody. Her first impulse, then, is to save her own skin, but whether she really means to tell or not, her words effectively set in motion the great scene of supplication, which scarcely could have taken place had she simply said at the start, "Rest assured, I won't betray you."

The scene itself is interesting from the formal point of view, in that it is cast into two set speeches, with a choral tag between, which is the usual form of a Euripidean debate. But there is no debate. Helen and her husband are both pleading for the same thing, not against each other; and yet, the poet who had been able to turn the ἀντιλογίαι of Protagoras so effectively to dramatic ends has skillfully managed to give the scene the air of a debate, not through a series of opposed arguments, but through the same argument offered by two opposite personalities, with the chorus interposing, as in a real debate, the familiar remark tantamount to, "That was a good speech, but I am eager to hear what the other side has to say" (944 ff). There is no other side; the contrast is between the simple, moving eloquence of Helen where again, as in Iphigeneia's appeal to the chorus, intonations of a woman's voice echo unmistakably through the strict formalities of iambic trimeter, and the bumbling mode of Menelaus, an odd mixture of Gorgian reasoning and unnecessary platitudes about his own manliness. Yet again, he is not so ridiculous as might seem. His appeal to Hades to give back those who fell at Troy for his sake is extravagant rhetoric, certainly (969 ff); it is also another way of stating the vain guilt of war, together with an understandable demand that, now the truth has been found, some good should arise from it. But however differently the two suppliants present their case, the argument is the same: the argument from τὸ δίκαιον, justice, the return of a trust to its rightful owner, in the name of the honest and god-fearing King Proteus, who had received Helen in asylum. The scene did not have to reflect the form of a debate; Helen's speech alone would have been sufficient; but to put it thus emphasizes the conflict in Theonoe's mind as she listens, for she is debating with herself between what she has been ordered to do, and what she knows to be justice attended by mortal danger.

Her reply is as unique as her character and dramatic role. There is a controlled, though slightly tremulous, heroism in her words as she gives her decision in favor of Hera—not for a moment because of Hera, or because her knowledge of the divinities has led her to share in their sorrily motivated causes; she speaks only of the human cause which she calls piety, τὸ εὐσεβές:

> Piety is my nature and my will;
> And as I love myself, I will not soil
> My father's holy name, nor grant my brother
> A favor that will show me infamous.
> A vast temple of justice lies within
> My nature; this, my heritage from Nereus,
> I shall try, Menelaus, to preserve.
> I cast my vote for Hera, since she wills

Your good; for me, may Aphrodite be
Gracious, though she has never been my lot:
I shall endeavor to remain virgin always.
As to your reproofs before my father's tomb:
I say the same; I would be false, should I
Deny return; were he alive, he would have
Given her, yours to keep, and you to her.

(998–1012)

So far her words are simply a moral, almost legal, statement of Menelaus' right to regain his wife, and she
knows that she is supporting that right at her peril. Her
next lines are highly mysterious, and slightly reminis-
cent, both in their conviction and in their theological
haziness, of Antigone's defense of the laws of Zeus:

For there is retribution for such deeds
Among the dead and all men living: mind
Does not live in the dead, yet keeps immortal
Judgment, once fallen into the immortal aether.

(1013–1016)

Theonoe's meaning is, to say the least, elusive. The idea
that the mind of the dead maintains a kind of spectral
judgment upon the acts of the living may derive from
the hero cults (compare Aesch. *Choeph.* 324 ff, Soph. *El.*
836 ff, *Oed. Col.* 621 ff), but what of the aether, and the
mind falling into it? It has been well shown that Euripides here is making use of contemporary cosmological
theories partially, at least, developed from Anaximenes'
theory of Air as the substratum of all things. Theonoe's
words do vaguely recall Anaxagoras' doctrine that the
rotary motion started by Mind drives the hot, dry, light,
and rare seeds to the circumference of the universe to
form Aether (*Fg.* B 15, *DK* II, 40; see also Epicharmus, *Fg.*
22, *DK* I, 202; also *IG* I, 442, which perhaps reflects some
popular belief). The mind of man presumably consists
of such seeds, and thus may be said to "fall into the immortal Aether."

But there is more involved than cosmology and the eschatology of the mind. Aether in this play and perhaps elsewhere (see Eur. *Fgs.* 1023, 839, 877) seems to have a special significance for Euripides. The real Helen was whisked away by Hermes through the "folds of Aether" (44; compare *Iph. T.* 29), and, in an identical phrase, the phantom Helen disappears into it (605; compare 1219). The phantom was, of course, made of it (584; οὐρανὸς seems to be used synonymously at 34, compare Emped. A 49, *DK* I, 292). Now Theonoe, at her entrance, is performing purificatory rites in its honor, and she finishes by referring to it as to some kind of cosmic, universal principle. There is much truth in the observation that Theonoe invokes Aether (and πνεῦμα) as a source of something higher and more pure than the gods. Purity is regularly associated with Aether: Iphigeneia tells her dream to the Aether in order to exorcise it (42 f), and she purifies the statue of Artemis by bringing it out under the "holy Aether" before taking it to the sea (1177). Aether's regular epithet, σεμνός, among its sundry ambiguous meanings, includes the idea of purity. The *eidolon*, created out of Aether, was the means for keeping Helen's bed pure (ἀκέραιον, 48). But it was also the means to a gigantic deception by which the bloodshed at Troy became a mockery and Helen herself suffered seventeen years of exile and disrepute. Nor was this the only time that Aether lent itself to deceit. In the *Bacchae* (286 ff) Teiresias gives a dubious and sophistic explanation of the legend that Dionysus had been sewn up in the thigh of Zeus. Hera, it seems, had wanted to throw the infant god out of heaven, but Zeus fooled her by "breaking off a piece of Aether that enfolds the earth" and giving it to her to have her will of. This versatile Aether is apparently capable of becoming quite substantial, in fact the opposite of itself. It would seem then that, while Aether may represent some higher purity and truth, the truth is paradoxical and includes no little seeming; Aether is the *primum mobile* of the delusive universe. Theonoe, who is in tune with it, must, as we have seen, allow the truth about Helen to come out by suppressing the truth about Menelaus and thus abetting a lie. Presently the lovers must complete the process by contriving an extravagant, almost preposterous, intrigue. Such a meaning does not seem to be beyond the powers of the great lover of paradox who could write, "Who knows if life be death or death be life?"

Theonoe departs bidding the lovers devise a plan of escape after praying to the two goddesses. She expresses the hope that by preventing her brother from an unholy act of murder she may make a better man of him (1020 f), but she must also foresee the opposite (see 893). She has in fact committed an act of self-sacrifice, responding to Menelaus' and Helen's determination on suicide. There seem to be limits to her clairvoyance. She does not give any hints about how to escape, nor does she say whether or not any plan will succeed. One might say that if she had there would be no need for the last third of the play. That is true, but it is also true that Theonoe's decision has altered her relations with gods and mortals. Helen had said that it would be shameful for her to have divine knowledge of past, present, and future and yet know nothing of justice (922 f). By choosing justice Theonoe has chosen the side of humanity, and at risk to herself; she has joined the world of dubious outcomes, and her mistaken remark about improving her brother is probably intended to indicate that she is no longer the detached holy seeress with total insight and foresight who entered purifying the air, but has become a woman who can understand human suffering and become involved in it. One feels that when she leaves she is a little less in touch with the gods, and perhaps a little more with the ambiguities of the Aether.

So far the lovers have had luck, and their first act has succeeded. The tone now becomes palpably lighter as the real intrigue begins. Menelaus makes two characteristically useless suggestions and Helen takes the lead. Her plan is, of course, an exaggerated revamping of Iphigeneia's, and far less plausible. It was one thing for Iphigeneia to persuade the superstitious, trusting Thoas that the statue of Artemis had averted its eyes from a matricide and that it needed special, secret lustrations. But to have Helen persuade the King that Menelaus was dead, on the word of one shipwrecked survivor, that she had instantly changed her mind and was ready to remarry, and then to swindle him out of his best new ship in order to perform bogus funeral rites that he had never heard of—this calls for a real fool in royal robes. Yet Helen is Helen, traditionally a bit of a sorceress and certainly irresistible. Moreover, as said earlier, the basic mode of the play is romance, which tends toward extravagance, and when one thinks of the wild, unlikely devices and tricks that strew the pages of, say, the romance of Tristan and Iseult, Euripides seems mild. Menelaus himself, at the expense of dramatic illusion, remarks that the idea of pretending to be dead has something old and stale about it; after at least three, and who knows how many other versions of the Orestes legend, all involving the same ruse, he might well say so, though the motif of assumed or alleged death was later to become an accepted convention of romantic drama (Imogen, Hermione, Perdita, Juliet, and so forth). But Menelaus' ironical undercutting of this crucial part of the plan shows that Euripides is not setting too much store by the techne of the play, that the outcome is almost perfunctory, once the real essence had been dramatized in the scene with Theonoe. Menelaus' clothes are again mentioned, to assist in the stratagem, and to point thematically to the successful event:

> *Men.* Indeed, these rags that gird my body round
>   Will bear witness with me that I was shipwrecked.
>   (1079–1080)

The rags can now serve as a practical means to salvation after suffering, and in fact they do impress the King sufficiently to convince him that Menelaus is a shipwrecked mariner, as of course he is (1204). Truth works in the service of deception, as the motive power of intrigue shifts from Hera, the contriver of the original illusion, to Helen who will bring the plot full circle.

As for Theoclymenus, he is not only a fool, he is also a villain, a villain with a peculiar touch of piety toward the tomb of his dead father, whose will he is diametrically transgressing. Thoas too was pious in his way, but he was at least consistent with himself and not wholly unsympathetic. But Theoclymenus commands no sympathy, a paper character designed merely to provide the final obstacle. Yet in one odd passage this violent man sounds the note of purity:

> My house is stainless, for it was not here
> That Menelaus perished.
>   (1430–1431)

He seems hypocritically relieved to be clear of the murder that he certainly would have committed given the chance; a "fugitive and cloistered virtue." Theoclymenus is probably Euripides' invention, as Theonoe (or at least her name) almost certainly is, and meant to stand as her moral and religious antitype; their two names at least support the suggestion: Theonoe, "of godly mind," Theoclymenus, "of godly reputation," real versus apparent piety (compare 9–10, if genuine).

Before he enters, however, the chorus sing the ode on
the misery and folly of war (1107 ff). But the second
strophe is the climax also of the main theme of inscrutability, both of the gods and of the affairs of men:

> Whatever is god or is not god, or something between,
> Who of men can say, though he search to the farthest
>   limit,
> When he sees the ways of the gods
> Leaping hither and thither
> With contrary, unlooked-for events? (τύχαις)
>   (1137–1143; compare 532 ff, 711 ff)

They then give the example of Helen and her phantom,
and conclude, in lines whose true readings are unfortunately in some doubt:

> I cannot tell
> What clarity ever exists among mortals;
> But the word of the gods I have found true.
>   (1148–1150)

The last line strikes one as at odds with the earlier ones
about the impossibility of knowing anything about the
gods. But the meaning may be simply that there is no
sure way of finding out what the gods are up to unless
they reveal it directly themselves; this would accord
with the Messenger's earlier denunciation of seers and
prophecy, to which, however, he adds that one should
pray and sacrifice to the gods (744 ff). This doubt about
the value of prophecy, combined with the feeling that
the gods can make clear what they wish, appears in
Jocasta's famous lines in Oed. Rex (723 f), and becomes
something of a commonplace. But the gods make themselves clear only after the event, after the human passion and struggle has somehow haphazardly completed
itself. Meanwhile, all is darkness save for vague signals
that are usually misleading. Perhaps this is why the ode
mentions Nauplius (1126 ff), and why Menelaus men-

tioned him earlier (766 f). Nauplius, in revenge for the murder of his son Palamedes, had set false channel lights off Euboea to wreck the Greek fleet on its return. Euripides' stress on this minor event of the *Returns* suggests not only that experience is deceptive but also that a deliberate malignity lies behind the deception. After all, Hera's original forgery was deliberate. Life is a night voyage into false channel lights.

And yet the lovers survive. If the gods can connive, so can human beings, and the intrigue works. It works rather slowly. In contrast with the *Iphigeneia*, where the gulling of Thoas is accomplished in a single scene of 80 pointed lines accelerated by broken tetrameters toward the end, it takes two scenes totaling 216 lines, all in iambics, to get Theoclymenus into the net and the lovers off the stage. The two scenes are needed, so that in the interval between them the offerings may be prepared and Menelaus may at last be decently dressed. But for the climax of an escape plot, the pace is somewhat leisurely; there is no desperate suspense, and the verbal interchanges lack the brilliant irony of the *Iphigeneia*, though there is some. The plans are, of course, for a funeral, and Helen's feigned grief might seem, perhaps, to render haste inappropriate to the dramatic fiction. Even the final departure from the theater must have taken some time, if the choregus actually staged, as he almost must have, the horse and the bull, the chief mourners, the offering bearers, and the crew of rowers for the Phoenician galley, in a solemn, ironical procession. One feels that the poet was not greatly interested in the action of this play, as such. But the *Helen* is less melodrama than romance, and Euripides, shaping instinctively what were to become the conventions of the mode in drama, dispensed with high tension, and allowed his plot to unravel in scenes of relaxed, almost casual make-believe, supported by spectacle.

Between the two parts of the deception comes the mysterious ode on the Great Mother, generally considered the most irrelevant ode in Greek tragedy. The chief sources of difficulty lie in the last stanza, whose opening lines tax Helen with neglecting the rites of the Great Mother and thus incurring her wrath; the closing lines are hopelessly corrupt. In between are some lines extolling the orgia of Bacchus and Cybele, here identified with Demeter. It seems impossible to untangle the details; precisely why and in what way Helen neglected the Great Mother and how that fact, if it is one, relates to the play is obscure. If the text of 1353 f is correct, she seems to have made a burnt sacrifice of some unlawful items, but one can only conjecture what that has to do with the substance of the ode, Demeter's search for Persephone. In a general way, however, Helen can be, and has been, seen as a human counterpart of Persephone lost and recovered; the poem then is a song of death and resurrection, solidly attached to the play as a whole and following quite logically on the scheme of the feigned death of Menelaus. Also, Euripides knew that Helen was worshiped in Sparta as a goddess (Or. 1635 ff, 1683 ff), doubtless of vegetation, and he may even have intended to hint at a momentary identification of her with Kore. The syncretism of Demeter and the Great Mother had already taken place by the late fifth century, and Euripides seems to have made use of it here so that he might introduce the wild, orgiastic music that attended the rites of the Great Mother. Zuntz finds the essence of the ode in "music redeeming life." Certainly the deathly music of the Sirens in Helen's first lament has given way to songs of the Muses and the tympana, flutes, and tambourines of the Great Mother, in celebration of life's return. Zuntz also stresses, rightly, the fact that the mourning Demeter is finally made to smile not by the obscenities of Baubo, as in the Orphic fragments, nor by the politer jestings of Iambe of the Eleusinian tradition, but by the Graces, the Muses, and Aphrodite. The point is that, after long waiting and suffering, a saving touch of grace may come, here symbolized by the music of the goddesses who preside over harmony and the joy of life. It is a pity that the final stanza cannot be really clarified, for the poem is one of the most vigorous and beautiful in all Euripides.

The closing lines of Menelaus' prayer to Zeus are explicit about the need for the touch of grace:

> I ought not to fare ill forever
> But to walk upright; grant me this one grace,
> And you will make me blessed ever after.

(1448–1450)

Menelaus' tone has changed; it is firmer and more dignified, as befits a man taking a bold step in a desperate hour. We begin to recognize, in fact, more of the Menelaus of the *Iliad*, and less of the Menelaus of the *Odyssey*. His prayer balances that of Helen to the two goddesses (1093 ff), where her appeal to Aphrodite, "Let me die, if it is your will to slay me, in my own fatherland," strongly recalls the celebrated prayer of Ajax in the *Iliad*, "O Zeus, if it is your will to slay the Achaeans, slay us in the light (XVII, 645 ff)." Euripides seldom exploits heroic values, but if the moment of truth is to come, it calls for a high-spirited effort and a drop of grace, as well as for strategem and intrigue.

The kind of intrigue that we meet with here and in *Iphigeneia*, designed to bring about justice and put all things in a true light, is a device for creating form and artificially imposing it on a world warped and made shapeless by networks of illusion. But form implies wholeness and purity. For some seventeen years Helen had been, in a sense, two women, her real self lost in the limbo of Egypt, her imagined self universally cursed for

sins never committed by her. On another level, Menelaus' misfortunes had reduced him to a feeble echo of
himself, a thing of "looped and windowed raggedness,"
calling for his lost armies (453). His problem is fairly
simple: given decent apparel and a chance to show his
valor, he recovers promptly. But his action is only the
completion of Helen's plan, which is the real action, the
real vehicle for achieving wholeness and form. And it
is important that it be hers, for though she was innocent
of adultery it was through no effort of her own; Hera's
whim, motivated only by jealousy of Aphrodite, had
saved her from any struggle with temptation, and condemned her to years of helpless inaction. Theoclymenus
seems not to have been a temptation. True, with the
disappearance of the phantom, she had ceased to be two
women, but she had not as yet done anything, and true
wholeness demands ratification in act. She must act her
fidelity to Menelaus and prove that she has not kept his
bed pure only perforce. The plan identifies her with the
purity that was thrust upon her and makes it her own.
It involves elaborate lies, but that is part of the play's
basic paradox; truth is inseparable from fiction. And
again, purity itself seems inseparable from some form of
defilement and violence. Helen's purity comes about
only after the tragedy of Troy and the defilement of her
name throughout Greece. The pure Theonoe is commanded to assist in an act of murder, but refuses, tells
a lie, and is almost murdered herself for it. Finally the
struggle on the ship costs the lives of all but one of the
innocent Egyptian rowers. Life's "dome of many-colored
glass" admits light neither easily nor clearly, but it does
admit light; and that in itself is perhaps the charismatic
touch that sometimes makes salvation possible. The last
choral ode (1451 ff) begins by invoking the ship of salvation and imagining Helen's joyful return to Sparta; then,

moving through a series of air, cloud, and Aether images (1479, 1488, 1496), it ends with a prayer to the Dioscuri to protect the voyage and dispel their sister's ill fame, a prayer that is answered in the epilogue by the Heavenly Twins in person.

The frequently noted resemblance between the plots of the *Helen* and the *Iphigeneia* serves chiefly to emphasize the difference between the two plays. The plot is indeed the soul of the *Iphigeneia*, while in the *Helen*, one feels, it is there merely as a framework to support the interplay of a number of motifs and philosophic, or quasi-philosophic, reflections. The *Helen* is certainly a drama of ideas—perhaps too much so—though hardly a comedy. It has little, if any, of the theatrical impact of the *Iphigeneia*, being far less tightly constructed and far slower in pace. In drawing Menelaus, Euripides may have gone too far in exaggerating his traditional characteristics, and so made him a little more ludicrous than was suitable for the generally serious tone; like every bold innovator, Euripides may stumble on occasion. But whatever its dramatic shortcomings, the *Helen* remains a haunting poem. For its real beauty to emerge, it must be read thematically, with an eye to the recurrence and development of its motifs and symbols. If any classification is possible, one might call it a half-lyrical, half-philosophical romance. It has been compared, with some justice, to the *Magic Flute,* but the *Magic Flute* is a real farrago of the solemn and the hilarious. Perhaps a closer analogue would be *Cymbeline,* with Imogen as the faithful, exiled Helen, Postumus the brave but foolish husband, and Cloten as Theoclymenus. But there are no true analogues; the *Helen* is unique, as are all true works of art. We shall see in the next chapter how Euripides, using many of the same themes, could create a totally different drama in the *Ion.*

3

Ion

The *Ion* is the most affecting of the three romances. It is also the least suitably termed "romance," for, although it makes use of familiar elements, all foreshadowing the New Comedy—intrigue, the lost baby, recognition—it is lacking in the exaggerative implausibilities of the *Helen*, nor is it set in a faraway exotic land, but in Delphi. Though Delphi is represented as a place remote from the invidious contentions of the world, especially Athens, and a real haven of peace, still it is in Greece, not in Egypt or the Crimea. The conditions of romance are absent; and if one grants the assumption that there is a god Apollo who can violate a virgin princess, then the rest of the plot works to its conclusion through the agency of inevitable human passions, including fear, jealousy, vengeful rage, and some touches of unexpected but true and gracious intuition. The *Ion* is, in any terms, a genuine tragedy, and Euripides has appropriately returned to the statelier rhetoric of early drama; the intimate voice-tones, so inevitably detectable in the *Iphigeneia* and somewhat in the *Helen*, are not pronounced, though not totally absent from some of the heroine's speeches. For the most part, a traditional formality prevails, which gives to the play both dramatic seriousness and poetic sonority. The thematic texture is by far the richest of the three, and the themes, especially the basic ones of violence and purity, are more closely interwoven than hitherto, while the intrigues, of which there are several, dominate the action throughout, rather than serving merely to produce a successful denouement.

The *Ion* depends less than the *Helen* on the ambiguities of language and situation, and its structure is perhaps less tight than that of the *Iphigeneia*. But from the point of view of character and symbolism, it is far more organic, from beginning to end, than any other play by Euripides except perhaps for the *Hippolytus* and the *Bacchae*. The characters Creusa and Ion are conceived in full, tragic dimensions, whose scope and meaning are achieved and revealed through the guilt, struggle, and suffering that constitute the movement of the play.

Drama might be described as the art of finding oneself out. The way is long, but the truth, once found, vigorously transforms the past, present, and future of that most elusive of all entities, the self. In the *Iphigeneia* the discovery of the truth leads to happy redemption, while in the *Helen* there remains, even at the end, some doubt as to whether truth can ever exist without its *eidolon*, seeming. But the *Ion*, less philosophic than the *Helen*, and less beset by the plot's need for constructive action than the *Iphigeneia*, finds truth on a more solemn level than either, while not losing sight of the irony of persistent delusion. Also, while Helen is waiting for her husband, and Iphigeneia for her brother, Ion, before the play ends, is in search of himself, a fact that precludes the label melodrama.

There have been sad, even abysmal, misinterpretations. The play has been sometimes classified among Euripides' lighter works, without demonstration of where its levity lies. It has been called straight comedy. It has been called Sophoclean, without specification of its Sophoclean qualities. It has been celebrated, by Verrall and others, as a frontal attack on Apollo, Delphi, and Olympian religion in general, despite favorable words about Apollo at the end. It has also been found, with equal enthusiasm, to be a mighty defense of Apollo. Such criticism, assuming as it does that Euripides practiced each year to score a tendentious or intellectual point, ignores the nature of poetry, which in essence tends to embrace meaning and hold it in suspension, rather than to indicate a conclusion or prescribe a course. This is as true of Milton as it is of Wordsworth, or Wordsworth's work would be no more than a statement of the ennobling power of Nature, and *Paradise Lost* only an extended homily in disparagement of sin. The moral force of tragedy is a fact that does not turn a tragedian into a moralist, and Apollo's behavior in this play presents problems about the complex nature of divinity which are not to be resolved by any single stroke.

The version of the myth as Euripides tells it seems to be strictly an Athenian one. Elsewhere Ion is the son of the Achaean Xuthus and the Erechtheid princess Creusa (for example, *Schol. DV ad Il.* XIII, 685), but at Athens Apollo is his father, whence no doubt the cult of Apollo Patrous. The story is that Apollo found Creusa picking flowers near the Long Cliffs on the north slope of the Acropolis, dragged her into a cave, and violated her. She then bore Ion secretly, and exposed him in the same cave. Later she married Xuthus, who had helped the Athenians in a war against Euboea. However this version arose, it was congenial to the Athenians' vaunted belief that their nation's blood was free from all foreign elements, autochthonous, and uncontaminated by any intermingling with other peoples. It was better to have the eponymous hero of the Ionians a bastard than the son of a foreigner. Much is made in the play of these interrelated themes of autochthony and racial purity, which form a kind of exterior to the more basic themes of authenticity and internal spiritual purity.

As the play begins, Creusa and Xuthus, whose marriage has been without issue, arrive at Delphi to ask after the cause and what might be done. Creusa supposes that her child by Apollo perished, though some faint hope to the contrary still lingers. But the audience has learned the truth from the prologue, where Hermes tells the story of the rape and explains how Apollo had asked him to rescue the baby and its cradle and convey them to Delphi. There Ion, though not yet so named, has grown up as a temple servant, naively untouched by outside experience, ignorant of his parentage, and piously devoted to the god.

The plot unfolds in a series of intrigues that exploit the partial knowledge and partial ignorance of the three main characters. The first intrigue is Creusa's, and innocent enough: while her husband has stayed to visit first the oracle of Trophonius at Lebadea, she has come on a little ahead, in order to inquire secretly after the fate of the baby whom she exposed. She meets Ion and tells him the story, pretending that the whole affair happened to a friend of hers, on whose behalf she is acting. Ion is shocked by the tale and refuses to submit her question to the Pythia, or minister for her in a manner so discreditable to the god whom he serves. The next intrigue is contrived by Apollo himself, who, in reply to Xuthus' questioning, announces that the first person he meets on leaving the oracle will be his son. This, of course, is untrue, but Xuthus believes it, and Ion himself is at length persuaded. The final intrigue comes as a direct result. Believing herself bertayed, and wild with jealousy that Xuthus, but not she, should have a son, Creusa sends an old retainer to poison Ion with a drop of Gorgon's blood. The plot fails—it is left ambiguous whether chance or deity averts it—and Ion hastens to take vengeance. He is prevented from dragging Creusa from Apollo's altar, where she had taken refuge, by the Delphian Prophetess who had reared him, and this same priestess now gives him the cradle in which he was found, together with the tokens of his origin. These lead to his recognition by Creusa, his doubt and challenging of Apollo's paternity, and the final, stately apparition of Athena, who explains all.

Thus again, the plot is of the kind that Aristotle called the best, wherein irremediable crime is barely averted, as in the *Iphigeneia*. But its elements are more intricately involved, both among themselves and with the characters, who are more complex than in the other romances. For example, what might seem like a minor aetiological detail, the snake amulets customarily given by the Erechtheids to newborn children (21 ff), becomes involved, as shall be seen, with other serpent imagery of great importance to the play's movement, and symbolically as well with the characters of Ion and Creusa. The whole myth is also of a common aetiological kind, in which a god engenders the founder of a nation or familial line. But its treatment is unique. Pindar, for instance, in the sixth Olympian Ode relates how Apollo seized Evadne and begat Iamus, the father of a famous line of prophets. Such unions of gods with mortal women, being in a sense no more than ethnological aitia, were looked upon as divine appointings, orderings of the way things are, and evidence of the gods' imperious but beneficent interest in the events of the earth. Pindar tells Evadne's experience in lofty words: "There at Apollo's hands she first met sweet Aphrodite" (*Ol.* VI, 35). Euripides, however, offers a different, less sanguine attitude. Immediately in the prologue Hermes describes

Apollo's union with Creusa, but not in any Pindaric
terms of divine afflatus coming upon a woman found
worthy: Creusa's case is simply criminal assault, and
Hermes' words are bleak and rough in the Greek, meaning literally "He yoked her with carnal violence." This
view is the one held consistently throughout, until
toward the end, and most vigorously emphasized in
Creusa's long and despairing lyric, where she tells her
story in full. We are invited, or rather compelled, to see
the whole action through the eyes of the violated girl,
helpless victim of a god's lust, who in terror of her
parents exposed her child to die. Her feeling that Apollo
should have saved him heightens her anguish and rage,
which reveals itself in a burst of tears as she first sets
foot in Delphi, and is greeted with such sympathetic
courtesy and admiration by the very son whom she
seeks.

Violation, then, is the keynote of Hermes' prologue.
Immediately juxtaposed in high contrast is the lyrical
entrance of Ion, a rapturous celebration of innocence
and the sanctity of Apollo's precinct. The sun is rising,
driving the stars "into holy night," and Ion has come
forth with attendants to cleanse, both physically and
ritually, the steps and forecourt of the temple. Words
denoting purity or holiness are heard repeatedly as he
conducts the proceedings:

> Come, O Delphian servants of Phoebus,
> Come to Castalia's silver eddies,
> And go sprinkling the sanctuary
> With pure water.
> It is good to guard lips holy, reticent,
> And to show fair speech from every tongue
> To the oracle's eager pilgrims.
>
> Now to the tasks I have always done

> Since childhood on; with branches of laurel
> And sacred garlands I will make pure
> The ways of Phoebus, the ground wet
> With moist drops.
>
> (94–106)

Even the laurel broom with which he sweeps the steps comes from "immortal gardens where holy dews . . . moisten the sacred foliage of the myrtle," and presently he turns to sprinkling the lustral water of Castalia, "rising," as he says, "pure from bed." He is almost pathetically happy in his task, and prays that he may continue in it always (151 ff), content to think of Apollo as his father as well as the highest object of reverence. But Ion's temple service includes more than lustral water. He must keep the birds from defiling the shrine and the dedicatory offerings, and he does this with bow and arrows. As the birds begin to gather, he threatens first an eagle, "herald of Zeus," and then a swan, a bird sacred to Apollo himself:

> And here another, a swan floats down
> To the altars: move elsewhere, red-foot, on!
> Apollo's lyre and song together
> Will not redeem you from this shaft!
> Spread wing, pass on,
> And settle on the lake of Delos;
> Hear, or in bloody death
> Your last fair songs will flow.
>
> (161–169)

Purity, it would seem, involves bloodshed, which Ion duly performs as part of his service to the god who raised him (179 ff), though he feels some shame about it, since the birds bring messages from the gods—a delicate reference to the motif of knowledge. It is interesting that he says not even the lyre of Phoebus will save the swan from his arrows, thus introducing the lyre in close juxtaposition with the bow. Heraclitus had used both to illustrate his tension of opposites (*Fg*. 51, *DK* I, 162), but they are also opposites quite in themselves, symbols of harmony and destruction. Both instruments are attributes of Apollo, tokens of two of his principal aspects, and Ion is living up to both. His whole lyrical monologue is a carefully designed combination of .purity and violence, and can exist only for that reason. For quite apart from the irrealism of expecting a single man with a bow to prevent birds from defiling the temple, we learn in a later scene, doubtless designed to comment indirectly on this one, that doves were allowed the freedom of the precinct (1198 f). Indeed, it is one of these doves that, by drinking the poisoned libation, warns Ion of the plot against his life; and there is probably some deliberate irony in the fact that it is described as having red legs, as did the swan whom he threatened to shoot (163; 1207).

The parodos continues the counterpoint. As in the stretto of a fugue, the Queen's attendants admire in closer combination images of sanctity and monstrosity in the ornamentation of the temple. After a brief mention of Athena and the "fair glancing light" of the twin facades (if that is what the phrase means), their gaze fixes abruptly on a metope, presumably, of the Lernean hydra, and Heracles in battle with it, helped by Iolaus. Then come Bellerophon and the Chimaera, the battle of the gods and giants, with Athena overcoming Enceladus and Zeus blasting Mimas with lightning; and finally Dionysus slaying another of the "sons of earth." The temple at Delphi seems not to have been decorated with these scenes, and even if one assumes that they are dedications, it is no matter; what matters is Euripides' choice of them, and especially the culminating scene of the earthborn giant. All sound the theme of violence, and the most pertinent to the play as a whole is the theme of the earthborn. In the antistrophe, the note of sanctity recurs, but only briefly. The ladies ask Ion if they may enter the shrine provided they remove their sandals; but no, the shrine is too sacred to enter, even barefoot, without specified sacrifices; they must content themselves with looking at the outside and asking questions. And their first question is whether or not it is true that the temple contains the sacred omphalos, the stone that marks the center of the earth. Ion replies: "Yes; it is wound with fillets, and on each side Gorgons." Now, on other evidence it appears that the omphalos was flanked by eagles; no other author says anything about these Gorgons, so that it looks as if Euripides made them up. If he did so, it was because, in this play at least, the Gorgon embodied for him a particular symbolism. It is with a drop of Gorgon's blood that Creusa attempts to poison Ion, and later on we learn that the Gorgon was born of the earth. The word here should not be thought a textual mistake, as some scholars have done; Euripides wanted the earth's most sacred and central stone, bound with its holy fillets, to stand in the closest proximity with the most terrible monsters: purity and violence, truth and terror. One may recall, perhaps, the first scene of the *Eumenides* where the Furies have desecrated the Pythian shrine with their presence. But whereas Apollo drives out the Furies, the Gorgons are fixedly installed. The Gorgon-flanked omphalos frames the tightest possible image of one main strand of the play's meaning, the climax of all that has so far been mentioned; once it has appeared, the rest of the parodos is merely a transition to the first episode.

The meeting of Ion and Creusa introduces the other great theme of the play, the difficulty of achieving true knowledge. It was noted earlier that there was some evidence that Euripides was influenced by the cognition theories of Gorgias. Here the emphasis falls less on the problems of cognition itself and whether or not it is possible, and more on the pursuit of factual knowledge and, above all, the ability to accept and understand it. The *Ion* is thus somewhat akin to that most terrifying of all tragedies, *Oedipus Rex*. In the first place, all three main characters are in quest of knowledge; Ion himself is in quest of his parentage, and therefore he is, as seems to be inevitably implied by that quest, in search of true knowledge of himself. The play vividly dramatizes, among other things, the torturing difficulty of obtaining true knowledge, especially when Apollo, oracular god of truth, is of no great disposition to reveal it. "How will the god prophesy what he wills to conceal?" cries Ion (365; compare 373 f, 387 f, 390 f). The difficulty is multiplied also by the characters' own attitudes toward truth, their unwillingness to believe it when presented, or their actual terror of learning it. Ion himself, in his attractively innocent but callow youthfulness, is scarcely of the stature of the heroic Oedipus, whose insistence on truth was unflagging whatever consequences loomed. Rather, Ion's longing to know who his parents are is crossed with fears of who they might be. Near the end of the play, for instance, after all his ardent musings on his unknown mother, when he holds in his hands the cradle containing the tokens of his birth, he suddenly says:

> Now I will take this cradle to the god
> And dedicate it, lest I find a truth
> I want not; if my mother was a slave,
> Better let be in silence than to find her.
>
> (1380–1383)

The moment is highly characteristic of Euripides'

double, often multiple perspectives. There is in the
sweet young Ion a surprising, hardheaded reasoning
power and calculus of advantage that strongly qualify
his candor and warmth. Perhaps this makes his character a bit implausible; but his plausibility as a character
is of less importance than the way in which he illus-
trates the devious paths whereby one comes to knowledge. For actually, of course, he does open the cradle;
by an equally abrupt shift as the former one, he realizes
suddenly that he is caught beyond resistance in the
fatality of being whoever he is, and of finding out. But
the wavering was there; and it reappears as Ion starts
manfully toward the oracle to extract from Apollo a
clear statement about his alleged fatherhood. Greeted
by the epiphany of Athena in a blaze of light, he starts
back crying:

> Let us flee, Mother, lest we see the gods
> Themselves—

but then he stops, and adds:

> unless it is time for us to see.
>
> (1551–1552)

By such a marginal access of unexplained courage and
impulse toward truth does the truth sometimes appear.
Ion almost unwillingly uncovers a vein of magnanimity
in himself, by what means is not told, but perhaps by
what Plato called a "divine tyche," an intuitive good-
ness unaccountably present in a youthful soul. In one
way the situation is like Oedipus', in another just the
opposite. Oedipus drives single-mindedly toward a truth
which destroys him; Ion halts and wavers toward a discovery which is his salvation; yet for both it is the
beginning of a new and truer self. Ion's is the drama of
the first ananke of life, not the final, fatal ananke, the
basic rather than the ultimate necessity.

No less is Xuthus involved in the theme of knowledge—or, more properly in his case, of ignorance.
Xuthus—who is drawn more in the lines of a practical
Athenian burgher than of a heroic king—wants a son,
any son, and he does not care where he gets him from.
In his questioning of the oracle, he has shown himself
to be rather easily satisfied: Apollo had said that the
first person he met on leaving the temple would be his
son; Xuthus rushes forth, sees Ion, and with a great cry
of "My child!" tries to embrace him. The young man,
however, is considerably taken aback, not to say
repelled; he demands to know, when he has heard the
oracle, if he is supposed to be the actual son of Xuthus,
or if Apollo is simply handing him over as a gift.
Xuthus assures him that he is his actual son:

> Ion   How did such a thing occur?
> Xuthus We both alike may wonder that.
> Ion   Who, then, was the mother bore me to you?
> Xuthus That I cannot say.
> Ion   Did not Phoebus say?
> Xuthus I was so overjoyed, I failed to ask.
>
> (539–541)

Ion is less overjoyed, and less easily satisfied: he wants
to know what Xuthus had been doing some sixteen or
so years ago, and he pins his new "father" down in a
rigorous, rather embarrassing cross-examination about
his previous lovelife. Here again, Ion shows his strain
of hardheadedness in the face of a potentially powerful
emotional situation. Poor Xuthus, however, feels not
the slightest concern about which of his premarital
affairs might account for this piece of good luck, and he
acquiesces readily in the first plausible theory that Ion
constructs. It is perhaps not surprising that Ion recoils
from the thought of such a father, and is persuaded only
reluctantly to accept him. And even then, he makes a

long speech vainly begging to be allowed to stay at Delphi, rather than follow Xuthus to Athens. The whole scene has a certain humor, but it has its pathos too, in the dismay of Ion, and the simple-minded joy of Xuthus, who has, in fact, been deliberately deceived by Apollo. Nor is he ever to be undeceived, for Athena expressly commands that he be allowed to rejoice in his delusion to the end of his days.

"What is truth?" said jesting Pilate. The representation of Apollo as an arrant liar, not to mention his previous treatment of Creusa, has caused interpreters to see in Euripides' Apollo a mockery, a god who violates girls, then delivers a false oracle, and finally does not even deign to appear, but sends Athena to do his explaining for him. Admittedly, the deeds are there. And yet, though Euripides often treats the traditional figures of the Olympian gods to some novel interpretations, he seems here to have intended something more subtle than satire. We shall return to the other points in due time; but for the matter of the false oracle, it is well to keep in mind the nature of Xuthus himself. Xuthus, we have seen, is one who readily contents himself with what is offered to him, and is disinclined to conduct any searching examination thereof. Sir Maurice Bowra once said, writing on Greek religion, that "People get the gods they deserve." And this is perhaps the answer in Xuthus' case: Why inflict truth on a man who has so little concern with it? For it has been rightly observed that the delusion is in character for Xuthus; he gets, in a way, the "truth" he deserves. If this answer seems to be a denial of the very nature of divinity, it should be remembered that the gods of the Greeks were, in the view of Werner Jaeger, predicates of experience—deified images of the way things are.

In a play about knowledge, deception is a necessary

foil. One may recall that in the *Iphigeneia* and *Helen*, the solution of the plot and the rescue of the sympathetic characters are brought about by means of skillful and deliberate deception, not indeed by a god, but by two priestesses. In particular, Theonoe, whose name suggests a mind mysteriously in touch with the gods, reveals or conceals as she pleases, in truly oracular fashion. The gods with whom she is in touch are capricious in the extreme, but her action and especially her words about the "shrine of justice in her soul" suggest a kind of higher constructive relativism, as one might say, an ulterior range of truth; as if Euripides were groping toward a hint of random grace, and finding that the hard core, or "shrine," of justice can be attained sometimes by the suppression, or even perversion, of factual truth. Apollo then may not be the only oracular voice to manipulate some actualities in view of the characters involved, and in the interest of ultimate ends. The three romances present people, things, and events, to quote Christian Wolff, as strangely "transparent," "distanced" by a framework of totality that is in sharp contrast to the narrowly focused earlier tragedies of lust, war, and madness. The *Ion*, though the most realistic of the three, is no exception: it sees truth, purity, and knowledge as things not given, but achieved through action, length of time, and an approximation to the "distanced" perspective of the gods.

But it is really Creusa's search for knowledge that is the soul of the play, even as she is, despite the title, its central figure. Ion and Xuthus are both convincing, firmly drawn characters; but Creusa is an especial masterpiece. If she has neither the complexity of Phaedra, nor the barbaric force of Medea, yet she is a more rounded portrait of a woman than either, and certainly more appealing. As a type of helpless innocence violated by irresistible force, she might be compared with Hecuba in the *Troades*, or the *Hecuba*; but Creusa is still young, she still has hope, and it is the interplay between her frail, but lingering hope and her fixed knowledge of shame and loss that gives her character its bittersweet charm. Moreover, she has none of Hecuba's hoarse eloquence. Her knowledge, and the worst aspect of her suffering—namely, her rape by Apollo, and the exposure of her child—must remain secret. She has an air of aristocratic reticence; for though her part is a long one, taken in its totality, she speaks mostly in brief utterances, and Euripides, with great tact, has forborne to give her any long set speech. Instead, when she does, finally and openly, reveal her secret, she does it in a magnificent lyrical aria, with stunning dramatic effect, as the full passion in her soul bursts forth. Except when she is singing, her voice-tones are only faintly audible in comparison with Iphigeneia's, subtly muted in accord with her need for concealment. Seldom has Euripides so completely "felt" a character and allowed it to live its part without the intrusion of his own stylistic mannerisms or reflective concerns. Creusa is real in the best sense that a character may be said to be real, that is, perfectly realized as a poetic fiction. The tenderness and bitterness in her are mingled so appealingly that even when, driven beyond endurance, she plots murder, one feels that she deserves only to be consoled.

Ion himself, in his first meeting with her, feels powerfully drawn toward her, despite the fact that she speaks nothing but evil of his own god, Apollo. Perhaps this should be looked upon as instinctive filial feeling, which may work mysteriously even in ignorance, but it is also clear from his first speech that Ion is struck at once by her intrinsic qualities: her patrician bearing, and a beauty once sufficient to attract the eye of a discrimi-

nating divinity. More important, Creusa's quest for
knowledge is one that is interestingly involved with her
feeling toward Apollo: though she several times speaks
as if she were sure that her exposed infant died, yet she
has come to Delphi to inquire whether or not he actually did. It is clear that she regards Apollo's neglect of
the child as worse than his original assault upon her.
When denied access to the oracle, she cries bitterly:

> O Phoebus, now as then you violate
> My absent friend, whose cause I proffer here!
> You neither saved the child you should have saved,
> Nor will you, prophet though you are, reply
> To this his questioning mother.
>
> (384–387)

But at the thought that Xuthus may get a more encouraging reply, she says gently, and her voice-tones here
come tremulously through the verse:

> Loxias, if he wills
> Now finally to redeem his former wrongs,
> Might yet be friend, or, if not wholly friend,
> Still, what he wills as god, I will receive.
>
> (425–428)

Thus it seems that Creusa's whole evaluation of Apollo
and, indeed, her whole view of the meaning of the past,
rest entirely on whether the god has preserved the son
she lost, or at least, whether he will grant her a new
one by Xuthus. And when the truth is finally learned,
her words to Apollo have a strong magnanimous
breadth, as if now all the past were changed:

> Hear me too: I praise Apollo, though I praised him not
>   before,
> For the child, that once he disregarded, he has now
>   returned.
> Beautiful now are his portals and his oracle to me,

Hostile once; but now, upon the knocker of his shrine my
  hands
Cling in happiness, and joyfully I bid his gates farewell.

(1609–1613)

The past cannot be changed, but one may come to
understand it. Creusa has still the same knowledge,
only now she has it all. And perhaps, given the longer
perspective, it is not the worst thing for a woman to be
loved by Apollo, even if his approach had been somewhat elemental.

Creusa's search has also a further function: it eventually sets Ion's in motion. The young, sheltered temple
servant had often wondered who his parents were, but
had suffered no driving need to find out. Creusa asks
him, rather naturally (328), "Have you never sought out
your origins?" And we too are prompted to wonder why
he has not. His reply, that he had no clue or token to
go by, is not very satisfactory; for even though he had
no clue, it seems strange that a foundling youth brought
up in the very precinct of Delphi, and having a Pythia
for foster mother, should never have been moved to ask
the oracle who he was, or how he might find his
parents. Obviously, the plot offers one reason why he
could not have done so, and there is a suggestion (325)
that he may have feared, as he later does, to discover
that he was baseborn. But character offers the chief
explanation: Ion is a remarkably innocent young man
when the play opens, not wholly unlike Xuthus in that
he is not yet concerned to delve into mysteries. In his
utter ingenuousness, he has been content to think of
Apollo as his spiritual father (see 311), and he calls him
"father" in deepest reverence, never dreaming of the
ironical truth. He is simple and fresh as dew, and prefers
to stay that way. But Creusa's bitter words, and her
story of her supposed "friend," force Ion—not, indeed,

to inquire immediately after his own parentage—but to inquire after the nature of the god whom he serves, and to question the moral standards of divinities.

Moved by Creusa's tale, he promptly remarks: "The god has wronged her; the poor mother!" (355); later, when he is alone, he soliloquizes with all the moral earnestness of youth:

> Why does this woman in mysterious words
> Always riddle reproaches at the god?
>   . . . Does he betray
> Virgins with lust and violence? Breed secret
> Children and let them die? Oh, no, no!
> No, since you rule, prize honor! If a mortal
> Is evil-natured, the gods punish him.
> How is it just, you who write laws for men,
> You are yourselves answerable for anarchy?
> If all of you—which won't happen, but I put the case—
> You, Poseidon, and Zeus who rules the sky,
> Atoned to mankind for your rapes, you soon
> Would empty your temples paying for your sins!
> Preferring pleasures to sagacity
> You trespass, and no longer is it justice,
> If men reflect the gods' morality,
> To scold us, but the gods who teach us so.
>   (429–430; 437–451)

This is not the first time that Euripides had dramatized the problem of maintaining any moral validity in a world where the gods' own morality is under suspicion. Ion's indictment of Apollo is only a restatement, in terms of a young man's first shock, of the consciousness of divine irresponsibility that particularly marked the late fifth century. Sophocles seems often, though not always, to have surmounted the temptation to abandon belief in moral order by discovering it in the heroic spirit. Euripides, however, had little, if any, allegiance to the idea of heroism. On the other hand, his temperament was not akin to the religious indifference of

Thucydides, or to the acrid denunciations of all religion, morals, and law by the later Sophists. For him, the whole matter was a source of intense, incurable suffering, and it sometimes seems as if he felt that his function as a poet was to represent the old myths as archetypes of the disorder which he discerned around him. He certainly had no answer, and it is a mistake to overintellectualize him. For although Euripides clearly and frequently reflects the ideas and idiom of contemporary thinkers, there is no reason to think that he ever promulgated any systematic theory. Though his words constantly imply a sophisticated search for meaning amid chaos, his artistic stance is a deceptive one, an almost archaistic pose as simple storyteller. The lines that Euripides has put here into the mouth of Ion should not be thrust back into his own. They are a young character's partial expression of an uneasy doubt, not a religious manifesto by the poet; and this doubt, however widely felt it may have been in contemporary Athens, could find resolution only within the fictional structure of the play itself. There is no philosophic overlay, but rather poetic invention delicately seeking the essence of a myth, and rendering its contours into a synoptic harmony, complete only when the play is complete.

The first episode consists chiefly of a long stichomythy, which is carefully articulated into four parts, the three transitions being marked by allusions to Creusa's suffering (288, 307, 330). The questions exchanged between her and Ion in their first scene together function both thematically and dramatically. He wants to know everything about Athenian legend, and how Creusa's ancestors came out of the earth, or had chthonic associations, which he will shortly find he shares. She wants to know about him and his ancestry, a desire which is ironically identical with her own search for her lost child. Poetic theme and dramaturgy become indistinguishable in this moving episode. Distressed by Creusa's tears at seeing Apollo's "pure oracle" (243), Ion at length asks:

Ion	Who are you? Where do you come from? From what land Are you derived, by what name should we call you?
Creusa	Creusa is my name, the daughter of Erechtheus; Athens is my native land.
Ion	Ah, dweller in a famed city, and bred Of noble ancestry! My homage, Lady.
Creusa	In that much, stranger, I am blest; no more.
Ion	By the gods, is it true, as men allege . . .
Creusa	Well, stranger, what thing do you wish to know?
Ion	Your father's father sprang up from the earth?
Creusa	Yes, Erichthonius. Breed, no help to me . . .
Ion	And that Athena drew him from the soil?
Creusa	Yes, with her virgin hands. She did not bear him.
Ion	And gave him, as the pictures always show—
Creusa	To Cecrops' daughters to preserve unseen.
Ion	I hear the girls unsealed the goddess' box.
Creusa	Therefore they died, and their blood stained the crags.
Ion	Ah, well! What of this? Is it true or false, the tale—
Creusa	What tale is that? I have leisure in abundance.
Ion	Your father Erechtheus sacrificed your sisters?
Creusa	For the land's good, he dared virgin slaughter.
Ion	How were you only of your sisters saved?
Creusa	I was an infant in my mother's arms.
Ion	And did the earth in truth engulf your father?
Creusa	Strokes of the sea god's trident cut him down.

(258–282)

The earth gives, the earth takes away. But when Ion inquires about the Long Cliffs of the Acropolis, where the rape took place, Creusa bursts out again in anguish and rage, whereupon Ion, though mystified, tactfully changes the subject.

The next two series of questions come closer to the individuals involved, who they are and how they came to be where they are. When Ion asks after Creusa's husband, she does not at once give his name, but first explains that he is not an Athenian, but a foreigner, ἐπακτός (290), a word connoting stigma, and applied again later to Xuthus (592). Although her feelings toward Xuthus are reasonably kindly (977), she never forgets that he is an outsider, and at one place she even speaks of herself as if she had been taken captive in a war (298), rather than given as a royal prize to a faithful ally. But the affront to her Athenian pride is nothing to her grief at being childless, and when she says, with poignant irony, "Phoebus well knows my childlessness" (306), the line expresses not only the search for offspring that she shares with Xuthus, but also her secret search for her lost son. Ion's sympathetic response arouses her curiosity, and it is now her turn to question. "Who are you?" she asks; "How happy your mother must be!" The two sets of questions complement each other ironically, even as do the fates of the two characters involved, and Ion's story, closing with the remark that he has no clue as to who his mother might be, makes a natural transition to the fourth section of the stichomythy, in which Creusa tells her own story, disguising it under the pretext of its having happened to a friend of hers.

Ion's refusal to put Creusa's question to the oracle foils her private search, but her story has had considerable effect on this innocent, rather sanctimonious young temple servant who has been living out in his own behavior his idea of what Apollo is—as pure in word and action as what he referred to as Loxias' "pure oracle." (Ironical, considering what the next oracular pronouncement will be.) But Ion has much to learn, and his dewy freshness is gradually rubbed off him. After Creusa's departure, he tries to dismiss her from his thoughts and return to his holy lustrations, but then suddenly delivers the long, indignant expostulation, already quoted, on the wickedness of Apollo and the other gods (436 ff). Presently he is to be told that he himself is the illegitimate offspring of a casual, drunken encounter between Xuthus and a Bacchante—information discouraging to one's sense of Apollonian purity. When this misapprehension is cleared away, he is forced to acknowledge that his own great god has lied; later he also suspects that his new-found mother is lying, and that his father was really an ordinary mortal. It is interesting to note that Ion is not eager for the latter to be the case, and that the union between Apollo and the mortal woman, which he found so upsetting before, appears in a more hopeful light if he himself is the result. At least, when Apollo's paternity is finally established, Ion finds no fault.

No doubt there is some irony in all this; but there is something more cogent also: if this sensitive young man is to become the founder of one of the great branches of the Greek people, he must first, so to speak, become who he is; he must enter the world of his real engendering, and accept it. He must renounce his Apollonian life at Delphi, with its simplistic piety and its lack of commitment, where he has felt so complacently at home. He does not want to leave Delphi. Here, he says in his long *rhesis* to Xuthus, in a moment of fine self-admiration, he has been specially endowed by both "nature and law" with the quality that all men pray for: "uprightness before the god" (642 ff). He can still be innocent at Delphi; if he goes to Athens, which he calls καθαρά, pure (673), he will be a foreigner, that is to say, a defilement, as we learn from the many choruses that denounce him as such. A kind of mutual defilement seems implied: he will defile the purity of Athenian blood, while Athens, with its touchy passions and politics, will corrupt him. He does not want to go to the big city. But the big city has come to him, and the more he gets involved in its passions and the drive to act, the more he begins to partake of them, until he loses his innocence, once and for all, in the attempt on his mother's life. He does not, of course, know that it is his mother; all he knows is that she has tried to kill him, and his vengeful fury is such that he is all but willing to drag her from the altar and hurl her over a cliff, "tearing to rags her inviolate hair." The fact that he does not indicates that his piety is real, however unseasoned. We are reminded also that it was his sense of ritual propriety that had saved his life: when the libation had been prepared, one of the attendants by chance uttered a βλασφημία—an ill-omened word—and Ion had emptied the cup on the ground, with its poisoned contents, and called for a new libation. Evidently, the pious training of his early years is not a thing to be wholly rejected; but it is destined to be modified, sobered, and matured by some guilty involvement in action, the guilt of intended, if not actual, murder. Somehow, Ion has to work out in his own experience the kind of knowledge and self-awareness that will complete his character. It cannot be all Apollo's doing. And at the end, Athena's revelation only confirms something that, as he intimates (1608), he had already come to know.

With the entrance of the Pythia, Euripides develops the theme of purity in full explicitness. The prophetess who had reared Ion appears and orders him to refrain

from taking vengeance on Creusa. She says, "Go pure
to Athens" (καθαρός), and Ion retorts, "The man who
slays his enemies is pure" (1333 f). All that the prophetess means is "pure of bloodshed," and Ion's reply
simply echoes the legal claim that murder in self-
defense does not entail ritual bloodguilt. Furthermore,
he has legal sanction from the Delphians for executing
the would-be murderess (1223, 1256). But the word is
there, emphatically placed at the beginning of two con-
secutive lines. However, the prophetess has come not
primarily to rescue Creusa. She has come to give Ion
the cradle that contains the secret of his origin; the god,
she says, had just "put it in her mind." Whether her
words actually indicate the force of the divine or of
chance, the drive wheels of the universe are moving
dimly into view. The Pythia's injunction to "purity"
coincides with the gift of true and long-desired knowledge, knowledge of Ion's real identity, and she is
prompted thereto by Apollo, and also by what she refers
to as "the ancient law of the holy tripod." We are not
precisely sure what that law is: is it the necessity of
truth at last? In any case, the dramatic texture is immediately suffused with the coming of something deep,
lasting, and true. Are we now to think that there is a
purity that is not at variance with knowledge, that real
truth is in itself pure and purifying, however it may
alter youth's innocent vision? Something of the sort
seems implied, and we are now prepared for the splendid recognition scene. When that is finished, we see a
new Ion; the sanctimonious boy is gone, and a real
young man is ready to enter upon his life. The motifs
of purity and knowledge have interlaced, and a new
range of meaning is added to each.

Yet what, one may fairly ask, has this kind of knowledge to do with purity? Has not Ion's access of

knowledge entailed, in fact, loss of purity? It has certainly entailed loss of innocence; but the two are different. Innocence is what is necessarily lost by action, and purity is what must be found by suffering and knowledge. In the Greek text, it is true, there is no verbal distinction, since the words used all come from the vocabulary of ritual and law; but the distinction is implied in the way in which these words accompany the motifs of knowledge; it is implied as well throughout the action, and especially in the symbolism of the unfading olive, which crowns the recognition scene. Purity in this sense is akin to what is sometimes called authenticity. It is, in any case, a kind of spiritual wholeness, which comes upon a person when an experience, of grave and threatening dimensions, has been lived through in all its active and passive phases, and comprehended at last as the shape and token of one's being. Perhaps there is no very adequate term for it, in English or Greek. It has been argued, by Gerald Else, that Aristotle meant something very like it by his much-disputed word "catharsis," to indicate a hero's recognition of truth hitherto obscured by his state of ignorance, or hamartia. It should be added that the term catharsis also stems from legal and religious contexts involving blood-guilt, and that in itself it suggests nothing about spiritual wholeness. But in this particular play, as in others too, where the Recognition establishes the truth of the hero's identity, and his final acceptance thereof, the meaning of "purification" may be implicitly extended, in that in becoming his true self, the hero has finally become really pure ($\kappa\alpha\theta\alpha\rho\delta\varsigma$), as gold is pure when unalloyed.

In any event, Euripides has filled this play with images of freshness, innocence, and purity, interweaving them with other images—and deeds—of experience, knowledge, defilement, and violation. This is not uncommon for Euripides; shattered innocence is a frequent theme in most Euripidean drama, and there is usually no redemption. The *Ion* is unique in its discovery of a deeper kind of purity, something inviolable that outlasts the pollution of experience and is able to emerge only because of it. Throughout, the images of purity and pollution are too numerous to list. We hear how the virgin daughters of Cecrops were cast down a cliff for opening the box in which Erichthonius was concealed; we hear of how Erechtheus had sacrificed his daughters to save Athens in a war against Eleusis; we are constantly reminded of the purity of Athenian blood, and the threat to it from outsiders, either by marriage or by invasion. Above all, of course, there is Creusa, Erechtheid princess, purest of the pure Athenian blood, but violated by Apollo as she was gathering flowers near a sacred cave. Even Creusa's hair, when she is threatened with having it torn out on the rocks of Delphi, is described as "inviolate."

The course of Creusa's experience parallels that of Ion, though the process takes longer. Her innocence has long been lost, and she has had the intervening years of shame and anguish over the child and its presumed death. But true knowledge is a brave elixir, and by the end of the play, Creusa has not only made her peace with Apollo; she has—what that peace means—become a whole woman. True, there is still a reservation; Euripidean skies are seldom wholly bright: she is told that she must never reveal that Ion is her son. But now the former torturing, untellable guilt and rage have become a kind of secret, sustaining knowledge, a true consciousness of what she has really endured and accomplished—in short, of who she is. And again, the moment of final revelation is attended by one of the most triumphantly lovely symbols of true purity in all poetry. In the recognition scene, Creusa sees and knows the cradle, and cries

out to Ion that he is her son: Ion, with the open cradle
before him, challenges her to name the tokens without
seeing them; and, with her life hanging upon her success, she does. The first two are quite expectable; there
is a sampler, and some snake amulets. But the third and
last token is a wreath made from Athena's own sacred
olive tree on the Acropolis:

> Creusa An olive crown I gave you, from the tree
>   That first Athena planted on her rock.
>   If it is there, its freshness never fails,
>   But blooms still, born of the unblemished tree.
>   (1433–1436)

It is as if all were suddenly given back, in greater abundance than before; and the poet has limned this flooding
restoration in one swift image of what Hopkins calls
"the freshness deep down things." Incapable itself of
fading, the immortal olive branch has not allowed even
the cradle to molder in time. The child did not die, and
Creusa has found him; both are made whole, both purified, she of her dark and guilty memories, he of his
murderous intention, both of their ignorance. Purity,
perhaps, like the olive wreath, is what was secretly there
all the time and must only be learned. And by contrast
with the two main characters, Xuthus remains rollick-
ingly untouched by any access of understanding; deceived, but unquestioning, he has, in fact, kept his
innocence.

The odes of the *Ion*, apart from Creusa's great aria, are
perhaps less striking than those of other plays, but they
parallel the thematic structure of the action. The first
(452 ff) is a song in praise of fecundity and a prayer that
the Erechtheids may encounter "pure prophecies of fair
issue." But the poem begins rather curiously with an
invocation to Athena and Artemis who, as sisters of
Apollo, might bring their influence to bear. Although

Artemis in one of her aspects can be a goddess of fertility, that aspect is rare in Attic legend, and in the present dramatic context it is her virginity, as well as Athena's, that is stressed. In Athena's case, further emphasis falls on the peculiar circumstances of her birth from the head of Zeus, and the fact that she was born without pang of childbirth and without the aid of Eileithyia (452 ff). These two goddesses seem to have been chosen, not as divinities who preside over fecundity, but rather as images of inviolate, sexless purity, even as they were associated in the *Iphigeneia* for a similar reason; and it is certainly no accident that their presence at the beginning of the ode is balanced at its end by an apostrophe to the Long Cliffs and the haunts of Pan where Creusa was ruthlessly deflowered by Apollo. While the main part of the ode arises from the immediate situation as developed in the foregoing scene, the beginning and the close are derived from the thematic burden of the total play.

The second stasimon (676 ff), following the scene between Ion and Xuthus, contains some textual difficulties, but its meaning is clear. The Queen's ladies cry out in indignation against Xuthus' betrayal of her; but there is something even worse. Not only has Xuthus found a son and the Queen not, but the son is an alien, as is, of course, Xuthus himself (702 f). They consider Ion a "foreign invasion," and end by praying that he may die before ever setting foot in Athens (719 ff). This climax in part motivates the scene to come, in which Creusa and her old retainer frame the plot to poison Ion; more important, however, is the reversion to the theme of Athenian autochthony and racial purity, which provides the context of the third stasimon (1048 ff), an extended *defixio* against both foreigners, and a prayer for the success of the conspiracy.

This cherished belief of the Athenians included a number of aspects, which Euripides exploited to great dramatic purpose. One was that they were sprung literally from the earth itself; another, that they had never been driven from their land, which seems to be true, or mingled with other peoples, which certainly was not. The principal story was that their remote ancestor Erichthonius had been drawn up from the soil by Athena (with virgin hands, as Euripides says; there are numerous references to virgin birth, 109, 270, 453, 503, where Creusa is called παρθένος τεκοῦσα), and delivered to the daughters of Cecrops, sealed up in a box together with two serpents as bodyguard. From these serpents Athenian mothers derived the custom of placing gold snakes as amulets in babies' cradles, as, of course, Creusa had done. Erichthonius was worshiped as a benignant earth hero and the very personification of Athenian autochthony.

All this was pure Attic legend, and Xuthus, who is an Achaean, does not believe a word of it (542); neither, of course, did Euripides, literally, that is. Why, then, is there so much made of it in the play? One may say, in the first place, that the image of a holy secret, sealed in a chest, is a motif that fulfills itself in the crucial recognition scene when the cradle is opened and the sacred olive wreath discovered. Ion was more fortunate than the daughters of Cecrops who were blasted for opening the box containing Erichthonius; but, perhaps, the probing of ultimate secrets may lead either to salvation or to destruction. Sophocles in the Oedipus plays saw it as leading to both. There is a further point, one involving some ambivalence about purity of blood, and the meaning of being "born of the earth." Erechtheus, it will be remembered, sacrificed his daughters to prevent an Eleusinian invasion, and consequent pollution of the race—a clear example, again, of innocence violated to preserve a kind of purity; so too, the chorus joins enthusiastically in Creusa's plot to poison Ion because he threatens the purity of the Erechtheids. Clearly, this prized notion of purity prompts some dark deeds; and, not so differently, the idea of being earthborn has two aspects. Heroes, like Erichthonius, are born of the earth, but so too are giants and sinister monsters, such as the Gorgon, whose blood Creusa carries in her bracelet. Now it should be observed that the Gorgon is an earthborn creature only in this play; normally, as in Hesiod, she and her sisters are sea monsters, daughters of Phorcys and Ceto, and they have continued as such right into modern Greek folklore. The usual story was that when Perseus had killed her, Athena collected her blood and gave it to Asclepius, the blood that flowed from her left side being a deadly poison, that from the right a powerful healing drug. (Apollodorus III, 10.3.) In Euripides, the story is that the Gorgon was born of the earth, at the battle of Phlegra, to help the giants against the gods; that Athena slew her and gave two drops of her blood to Erichthonius, by whom they were handed down to Creusa (988 f; compare 1054 ff). There is also a Gorgon embroidered on the sampler which is Creusa's first token in the cradle (1421); so that the Olympian, eternally fresh olive wreath is accompanied by chthonic tokens, snakes and Gorgon. One is reminded also of the serpentine form of Cecrops at 1163 f.

Euripides has deliberately associated the idea of autochthony, in the literal sense of being sprung from the earth, with that which is monstrous, as well as miraculous, and has put the famous pure blood of the Athenians, and perhaps purity in general, into an ambiguous light. References to earthborn things are frequent in many plays of Euripides, and regularly associated with the more threatening sides of human nature. Thebes, for instance, had its race of Sown Men, who rose from the earth when Cadmus sowed the dragon's teeth; and in his late works Euripides uses them and their descendants as symbols of the destructive and brutal aspect of heroic force (for example, *Phoen.* 127 ff; *Bacch.* 538 ff, 995 ff, 1025 ff, 1155 ff). Whatever it meant earlier, by the late fifth century to be earthborn seems to mean to be something of a monstrosity; Aristophanes in the *Clouds* (853) refers to Socrates and his pupils as "earthborn." Earthborn things, and perhaps even Earth itself, are threatening: Ion invokes Earth when he appeals to the Delphic elders against the life of Creusa (1220), and identifies her with the Gorgon when he confronts her (1264; contrast 1529). And so it is appropriately with a drop of earthborn Gorgon's blood that Creusa, daughter of the γηγενέτας δόμος, earthborn house, proposes to murder Ion. But again, there is an ambiguity, an important one, hinting at the devious and perilous ways by which salvation comes, if it comes at all. There are two drops of Gorgon's blood in the bracelet, one that kills and one that heals; Creusa sends the murderous one, but it so turns out that it leads ultimately to revelation of truth and the survival of both mother and son. For mortals, the way of purity lies through violence and suffering. The gentle Creusa has twice tried to destroy the thing she wanted most, and the innocent Ion has tried to stone to death the person he most longed for. Both he and she are, in fact, earthborn; and, so, in an ironic way, they prove the purity of their Athenian heritage by being brought together in the end by a drop of earthborn blood. Not only the meaning of the olive wreath, but also that of the Gorgon and the snake amulets of old Erichthonius, have fulfilled themselves. Athena is the goddess of the mind, but she wears a Gorgon on her shield.

Somewhere on the fringe of tyche, by devices that

work somehow, Euripides brings his characters through to a kind of moral wholeness—*suum cuique*—with both irony and tenderness (see 1512 ff). There is too much tenderness, and also too much suffering, for the *Ion* to be called anything but tragedy. Moreover, there is the mystery of Apollo, which must not be dismissed as atheistical satire. It has been asked why Apollo sent Hermes to get the baby rather than getting it himself; also, most critics have felt that his failure to appear in person at the end and do his own explaining is less than morally responsible. No answer is given in the text to the first question, nor need there be, for to have sent Hermes is to accept the responsibility; as for the second, Athena says:

> He deemed unfitting to come face to face
> With you, lest old reproofs should rise again.
> (1557–1558)

This does not mean that Apollo is afraid to face the reproaches of two helpless mortals, as it is usually taken, but that reproaches for things done in the past have been superseded by blessings to come. Hence Athena, before whom a rehearsal of the past would not be pertinent, turns to the revelation of the future, a function that is as regular for the *deus ex machina* as it is for the prologuist to explain the past; the former troubles of Creusa and her son have now little relevance. Another, better reason for not allowing Apollo to do anything in person is to keep him, within the motion of the play, at a distance. His remoteness is important, for it parallels the remoteness of true knowledge itself, and contributes to the distanced perspective, through which alone totalities become visible.

"Oracles are steep," says the old retainer, meaning only that the path up to the Delphi temple is steep (739);

but his word for steep can also mean difficult and is so used by Pindar. Apollo's gift for obscure indirection is contained in his oracular epithet, Loxias, even as his radiant presence is contained in the epithet Phoebus. He is a god of many aspects, some apparently contradictory; he is god of truth, yet obscure and capable of deceiving Xuthus; god of morality, yet capable of rape; god of music and harmony, yet a destroyer. He bridges and unites many moral categories that are irreconcilable to the analytic mind. His terrifying union of beauty and violence is fully expressed in Creusa's aria, when she cries:

> O you who sing to the peal of the seven-stringed lyre,
> Ringing out echoing hymns of the Muses
> From lifeless horns of country beasts, O son of Leto,
> I shall proclaim your crime before the sky!
> Shining with golden hair you came to me,
> Gathering crocus petals into my gown's fold,
>   Decked with their amber glow:
>   You, O god, seized my white wrists,
>   Dragged me and bedded me, crying "Mother,"
> There on the cavern's floor, ruthlessly
> Doing the work of Cypris.
>
>   (881–896)

And she ends by saying that Delos, his own holy birth-place, with all its laurels, hates him (919 ff); yet he wrings music from lifeless things. Apollo is quite as full of contradictions as Artemis was found to be in the *Iphigeneia*, but by contrast, the *Ion* does little to resolve them, leaving the god instead in the familiar tragic perspective, mighty, mysterious, aloof. If he can violate, and shoot arrows that deal pestilence, yet he is also the god of healing; appropriately enough, it is in this role that he appears in the play for the last time:

> Phoebus has wrought all well, first that he kept
> Your childbed safe, that no one knew of it;

And when you bore the child, and cast him out
In swaddlings, he sent Hermes to catch up
The infant in his arms and bring him here;
Then nursed him up, and would not let him die.

(1595–1600)

There is suffering, there is also healing. Apollo is all
that he is. By no amount of argument can one force
or persuade him—or any other Olympian—to accom-
modate himself to the mold of the perfect drawing room
gentleman, nor should anyone try. Neither should the
happy denouement suggest the premise that from the
very first Apollo planned it all in just this way, as if
Euripides could see salvation as the result of a benignant, providential dispensation of grace. We know
nothing of Apollo's motivation except his very Olympian desire for Creusa; all that follows is techne or tyche.

It was suggested, at the beginning, that if Pindar had
told the story, a generation or two earlier, Apollo's union
with Creusa would have been a beneficent, only mo-
mentarily troubling, gift of divine afflatus engendering
the primal hero of the Ionians. For Euripides, viewing it
through the eyes of Creusa and Ion, it is a sadder, bit-
terer tale; but for all that, Euripides is not denouncing
Apollo and therewith all the gods. Rather he seems, for
once, to be almost vindicating them; that is, as far as
the gods of such a world as this can be vindicated. Euripides was certainly no lyrical celebrant of a divinely
ordered universe; but here, at least, he seems to have
felt that chaos, which includes just about everything,
might also include some random order, and that moral
survival may sometimes, somehow, be possible. In terms
of traditional thinking, his Apollo may cut a poor figure,
of course. But Euripides is not thinking in our traditional
terms, nor is he rejecting his own polytheistic tradition,
which had by no means yet been philosophized out of

existence; rather, he is using it. He is looking through
the big end of the telescope and therefore getting reduced images, no doubt; but the gods, it would seem,
and ultimately the characters, look through the other
end, and see things larger. The two who appear, Hermes
and Athena, summarize the past and future aspects of
the tale; we know that Apollo did not let Ion perish, and
we learn that Ion will indeed be a founding father, and
have a glorious career; while Creusa and Xuthus, as if
racial purity had been supplanted by spiritual purity,
will have legitimate children and all happiness thereafter. But the ending is not gratuitously happy; it is
simply that the telescope has been turned around, and
in the new perspective we are able to perceive the myth
as Pindar would have told it. Euripides, tragedian that
he was, dramatized the intervening suffering, the struggle of the human actors toward the moment of recognition and salvation. The struggle is hard, but the
moment does come. There is no predetermination of
events by high-handed deities, for Creusa's poison plot,
as Athena explains, forced Apollo to change his plans a
little; and one may recall that Creusa's beauty at the
outset compelled Apollo's passion. For the polytheistic
mind—for that is what Euripides had—the happenings
in this world result from interaction between human
and heavenly agencies; and these may meet, at last, in a
single, meaningful channel. If to suggest this is not to
assert universal order, it is to say that myth, enacted in
its fullest terms, leads ultimately to a certain valid
equipoise, whereby some individuals come to redemption and the joy of being their true selves. Far from dis-
missing or satirizing myth, Euripides found some breath-
takingly original ways to explore and use it.

4

The Scope
of Myth

Many a green isle needs must be
In the deep, wide sea of misery.

Amid his despair at post-Napoleonic Europe, Shelley, his mind as always on human redemption, wandered into the Euganean Hills and experienced in imagination a renewal of the world's youth, by way of a hazy vision of Venetian glory reborn, or else transfigured in a final sea change. History offers no answer to why, in the Athens of Pisander and Cleophon, with the echoes of the Sicilian disaster still sounding, and the city's ultimate defeat the only realistic prospect, the poet of the *Medea*, the *Heracles*, and the *Trojan Women* should have produced the three most reassuring plays of his career, at least as we know it. Escape has been the most frequent suggestion, and the most absurd. Apart from the discrepancy of the term with that other label, realism, so often applied to him, it is hard to see how Euripides could have sought, or the Athenians found, escape from their trials in these plays of suffering, misapprehension, struggle and barely won victory. Positive though they are in the event, they are far from lighthearted entertainment, and their moments of humor are simply not enough to construe them into comedies, in the New Comic sense. They are regularly, and perhaps rightly, looked upon as fore-bears of New Comedy, because they make elaborate use of intrigue, long-lost persons, and plots of somewhat far-fetched unlikelihood, but it is a perverse hypostasis to turn Euripides into a comedian because he developed themes that later proved productive—monotonously so —for comic poets.

There is nothing essentially comic about such themes. No plot is less likely than that of *Oedipus Rex*, unless it be the *Trachiniae*. Ion is not merely a lost child, he is a lost heroic child; one might say, a foundling father, destined for great things though raised in obscurity. As such, he fits far better into the myth of the young hero, of dual paternity and early years in exile, along with Theseus, Sigurd, and Zeus himself, than he does in the comic pattern of freeborn but mislaid children. The woman spirited away has her archetype in Persephone and her Near Eastern sisters, as Euripides made clear in the *Helen*; and as for intrigue, the last twelve books of the *Odyssey*, hardly a comedy in any later acceptance, provide venerable precedent. Mythic shapes, not comic gambits, are the springs of these three dramas, with all their tenderness, passion, and cloudlike detachment.

And yet, they inevitably contrast with Euripides' earlier and later works, all equally founded on myth. They rise like Shelley's "green isle" out of the murky chiaroscuro of lust, cruelty, and sheer madness that colors so many of the tragedies. What was this new vision of Euripides', and how did he come to it? If no promptings toward a drama of redemption can be found in the times, or in any circumstances known to us, yet the plays speak for themselves, as mythic structures of the poetic imagination, and their own best interpreters; for myth is both a commentary and the story it ex-pounds, narrative and interpretation in one. Seen in the

light of the myth that it enacts, the conventions that it
fulfills, and the characters created in the process, the
Ion, for instance, might be regarded as not, after all, so
great a contrast with Euripidean art in general, but
rather as a kind of culmination, or better, the most
rounded example of what that art includes. Throughout
his life Euripides dramatized myths, but always with
irony, sometimes as delicate as that of the *Alcestis*,
sometimes intensely caustic, as in the *Heracles*, so that
the mythic and ironic modes, to use Northrop Frye's
terms, seemed to strive in hopeless and irreconcilable
conflict, which suggested to many critics, ancient as well
as modern, the view so often repeated in the handbooks,
that the poet was satirizing the mythology of traditional
religion, demolishing clay-footed gods, and teaching reason. Yet the positive substance of Euripides' rationalism
has never been revealed by anyone, and its very existence has been devastatingly cross-examined by E. R.
Dodds, so that one is left with a sorry picture of the
poet destroying with sly malice something that he could
not replace with anything better, and, if Verrall could
be believed, taking a puerile joy in it. Nietzsche even
saw him as writing to please Socrates, and Socrates
alone, as if Socrates were guilty as charged, and Euripides his gifted accomplice in the dismantling of religion. That fantasy has faded, but the confusions linger,
and the question of what Euripides was really doing
with myth remains.

The trilogies of Aeschylus were mythic dramas in the
fullest sense of the word. Often, according to an ancient
account, he peopled his stage exclusively with gods, as
is certainly the case with the Prometheus plays, and
very nearly with the *Eumenides*. But even when the
characters are quite human, the import of their deeds
and suffering extends into the context of cosmic specula-

tion, and attains its final stage there. Every action, every word is a summons to the universe to respond. And it does respond in all its resonance and prismatic splendor, through masterful poetic rhythms and images as visionary as they are imprecise. The art of Aeschylus is agglutinative, after the fashion of epic; it aims at collecting within its scope no less than totality, as the great myths do, even though not all the parts may be logically assimilated. In such a scheme, irony's chief function is to reflect the discrepancy between the world process, as conceived, and the things men do as only partially aware participants in that process; men are identified with what they do, and the resolution of the conflict lies in the recovery of balance, as random human action, like a comet settling into orbit, finds a new and valid course within the universal ritual of moral order. The very emphasis on world process in such drama places it firmly within the mythic mode, even when a vitally individual character like Clytaemnestra threatens to give birth to psychological drama before its time.

Sophocles' dramatic scope, though not necessarily its implications, is far more restricted. Less mythic than Aeschylus in the meaning described above, he fixes his lens on a great individual of transcendent stature, a hero in fact, whose complex spirit, whole from the start, reveals itself in the brief temporal process of the play's action and, like the proverbial Spaniard, lives the life of the universe in one day. This mode—and we adhere to Frye's terminology—is the high mimetic, the mode of the single figure isolated in the merciless glare of crucial deed and thought. The basis of tragic irony here is the discrepancy between the hero's deed and his heroic self, the clearest example being, of course, Oedipus, who resolutely affirms that discrepancy to the citizens of Colonus throughout the first third of Sophocles' last play. This kind of irony seems to be Sophocles' particular own, but the mode is that of tragedy par excellence, and it returns in Shakespeare, Racine, and all poets who can focus their world view on individual experience as universal. Different as they are, both Sophocles and Aeschylus, whether through microcosm or macrocosm, offer a surmise of totality, a feat that became less and less a natural product as the years of the fifth century went on, and increasingly an "artifice of eternity."

When we look at the earliest preserved work of Euripides, we are struck at once by the lack of any such artifice. Myth is there in abundance, that is, mythic stories are retold and laced with allusions to other myths. Euripides is learned in the tradition; his mind seems to spin horizontally outward, as by some centrifugal force, to touch on tale after tale, motif on motif, whether as ornament, as something to be rejected, or as a remote explanatory cause. But there is no mythic artifice in the large sense to enclose this multiplicity, no intuition of a grand design, even if limited to the understanding of one person, as in Sophocles. Instead there is irony; not, in the early plays, internal irony coextensive with the dramaturgical forces of action and character, but the poet's own irony externally imposed, and ubiquitously corroding the mythic texture while the traditional structure remains untouched. Euripides could create neither cosmic nor heroic order. His mind swept over the kaleidoscope of mythology, choosing the little colored pieces for scrutiny, not estimating the total pattern in the tube but finding, quite honestly, that it is all done with mirrors; the pieces, however, were real, and he viewed them with the eye of a collector. There was genius in this ironic and disordered acceptance of the myths, for it meant that, whenever and if a vision of totality were to arise, it would give full measure to human and divine perversity as structurally inherent in the world. It would take account of small, contriving mortals; of gods remote and unregenerate, but indirectly drastic; and of the ambiguities of the irrational that works *per accidens*, but exists of an ineradicable necessity.

In short, it would be a vision of dramatic causality such as is found in the *Iphigeneia*, *Helen*, and *Ion*, where three motive forces, in constant interplay, become perceptible through the action: the effort of human characters, in the form of a plan or intrigue (techne, mechane), strives onward step by step, sometimes aided and sometimes thwarted by chance (tyche), while influences from divinity (daimon), whether as commands, oracles, deceptions, or epiphanies, play over both the rational and irrational elements of human experience with motley brilliance. The part of the gods, indeed, is sometimes difficult to distinguish from that of chance, for the gods confuse as much as they clarify; yet there is a felt difference in the enlarged perspective that they bring to bear, for divinity, though often in Euripides moved to action by the most dubious promptings, nonetheless is held to be sentient, where chance is not, and to be framed in the large dimensions of power and immortality. The gods need not be just, admirable, or even, perhaps, all-knowing; but they are always there, and Euripides invariably reckons with them as real forces in what might be called the motivational triad: techne, tyche, daimon. Often there is little discernible equilibrium in the working of the three; one or another may preponderate and the result may be the warped and tilted world so frequently thought of as typically Euripidean. But in the three late romances, the interplay works toward something like a harmonious wholeness, where most of the pieces, if not absolutely all, seem to construct among themselves a semblance, or hypothesis, of order.

At first, however, there were only the pieces, scattered

and disappointing. The *Alcestis* provides a good example
of how Euripides saw myth in 438 B.C., and suggests a
contrast with how he was to see it later. The myth is the
myth of Return from the Dead, which recurs, at least by
way of metaphor, in all three romances, and is basic
to all mythologies. Admetus, Argonaut and friend of
Heracles, was a figure of heroic legend, who had won
his bride by duly performing a princely impossibility,
and Alcestis was one of the great heroines. Out of love
for Admetus, Apollo had favored him with the privilege
of escaping death if someone else would die for him;
Alcestis sacrificed herself, but was restored by Heracles.
The legend was originally conceived, of course, as ennobling to all concerned. Euripides, without altering a
single detail, reduces all three principals to subheroic
stature: Alcestis, about whom the play might have been
expected to center, appears briefly and reveals herself as
simultaneously agonized by the loss of her children and
her own young life, and contemplating, with some detachment, her own nobility; she is little concerned with
Admetus, save that he should appreciate her and not
remarry. Heracles, slightly tipsy, rescues Alcestis as part
of the day's work and gives her back to her husband in-
explicably disguised. As for the protagonist, the virtues
of Admetus have been sought, but not found. A subtle
yet by no means ambiguous poltroon, he praises his
wife's sacrifice, and tearfully accepts it, only later to
wonder, amid his laments, what people will think of
him. He cannot understand his parents' unwillingness to
do his dying for him, and upbraids them mightily. By a
dexterous use of falsehood, he turns the famed hospital-
ity of his palace into an ostentatious farce, and when
Heracles, by way of reward, brings Alcestis back to him,
veiled and unidentified, he accepts her with reluctance,
again out of fear of what people will say. As for Apollo's

favor, like many of the gods' gifts, it seems to have done him harm, for it has convinced him that he is the most valuable person on earth, for whom all should be glad to consign themselves to the grave. Like the divinely favored Tantalus, he could not digest his great good fortune; he wears it with a kind of pseudo-godlike conceit, as if his almighty friend had granted him immortality, instead of a temporary stay. Could not Apollo, god of prophecy, have foreseen this? There is no reason to think that he could not, had Euripides chosen to deal with the matter; as the play stands, Apollo, like a true Olympian, seems to have simply confirmed the man in what he was, loftily toying the while with the human situation, as the prologue makes clear.

Surely the story could have been told differently; none of all this cool irony is native to it. Yet Euripides' haunting classic seems now so inevitable as to be the only possible rendition, despite the widely divergent constructions placed upon it. For some, perhaps because it stood in the place of a satyr play with the *Telephus* trilogy, it is a burlesque of heroic fiction, for others a "graceful masque," or a comedy; yet the language is too delicate for burlesque, and the prevailing mood, despite Heracles in his cups, is grave and tremulous under the palpable shadow of death. It has sometimes been classed with the romances, because of its happy ending, but the intensity of human struggle, the tilting matches with the gods, and above all, the wide speculative horizons of the romances are wholly lacking. The scene never extends beyond the palace at Pherae, Admetus makes no effort of any kind, and even Heracles' fight with Death is a simple, foregone victory in wrestling. Most important, the happiness of the ending is at least doubtful. When Heracles has unveiled the returned Alcestis, Admetus notices that she does not speak. Heracles ex-

plains that she must be silent for three days, until "purified before the nether gods." The language is vague;
philologists explain that the *Alcestis* was written for
only two actors, and therefore there was no one to speak
the part, an answer that makes one ask why Euripides
deliberately called attention to this limitation, especially
when he had already introduced one supernumerary to
sing the part of Eumelus. Heracles' reason is said to be
supported by a popularly alleged regulation for reve-
nants, but the evidence is scarce. The dramatic point of
Alcestis' reticence is clear and effective: she has nothing
to say. What could she have to say to the husband who
assured her, in all his devotion to her beauty, that he
would have a statue of her made, to place beside him in
bed? Heracles' words, as he hands her over to him, are,
"You have everything that you wished for," and one is
driven to feel that this Apollonian beauty-lover's desires
have indeed been well fulfilled in the receipt of something very like a statue. Apt comparison has been drawn
with the close of *A Winter's Tale*, another play called a
comedy, though it contains far less to laugh at than
Hamlet. The "statue" of Hermione does speak, but exclusively to Perdita, and not a word to Leontes. In the
austere Greek version, the returned says nothing at all,
with a presage of silence for the remainder of a lifetime
to come.

The *Alcestis* is tragedy, tragedy of the Return from
Death to Death in Life, and Euripides has cast a cold
eye on both; it is also tragedy of the self-fascinated ego,
and of its resulting blight on human nature. But it is not
high mimetic tragedy, for it explicitly rejects the heroic
individual, while retaining the mythic tale which was
originally identified with a hero. Throughout his life,
Euripides made use of heroic fiction, without ever shaping a heroic figure, and by so doing he laid the founda-

tions of a persistent misunderstanding—in which he was helped no little by Aristophanes—to the effect that he had degraded the art of tragedy to a daily household level, in which maidservants, clever schemers, and decrepit old men replaced the grand figures of yore with an intolerable volubility as lacking in poetic elevation as it was in the moral virtues. Like most of the half-truths about Euripides, this hardy perennial confuses things that he did not do with things that he did. True, he allowed more scope in his theater to characters of low social status, some of whom are splendid creations: probably the most moving single speech in the *Alcestis* is the slave girl's account of her mistress' farewell to her household (152 ff); certainly a crucial speech to the plot of the *Ion* is the doddering old retainer's analysis to Creusa of her husband's betrayal (808 ff). Medea's, Hermione's, and Phaedra's nurses, Electra's farmer-spouse, Antigone's pedagogue, and sundry philosophizing messengers all illustrate the frequently uttered maxim that slaves can think as well and as nobly as the freeborn. With extreme artistic self-consciousness, Euripides transplants quotidian characters, native to what Frye calls the low mimetic mode, into the world of myth, to breathe its air as best they can in company with their reduced masters.

What Euripides did not do was abandon either the framework or the implications of the myth in which all these characters move. The framework continues to surround them, slaves, minions, and demythologized heroes alike, and the overtones are still those of the wide universal world of the grand tradition. The result is a jarring discrepancy of ethos between the two factors, a kind of deliberate polytonality, as if tragedy were now being written in two keys at once. This is precisely the manner of irony, and it should not be confused with the low mimetic mode, though such confusion occurs in the above-mentioned criticism by Aristophanes and others. The low mimetic is the mode of the novel and other forms of realistic and quasi-realistic representationalism; it creates its own illusion, recognizable as true or false by its degree of resemblance to the familiar, everyday experience of the reader; its power lies in the immediacy of its mimesis in the strictest sense, and its metaphysical dimension is practically nonexistent. Irony, however, has a metaphysical dimension, in that it supports the simultaneous existence of contraries in a single capsule of meaning, be it word, image, or entire work of art; and the creator of such a capsule always betrays his presence, which is why Euripides' personality is felt in his plays much more strongly than is Sophocles' or Aeschylus'. He constantly reminds his audience that he is making what they see before them, whereas the two earlier poets foster the illusion that the mythic tale is creating or re-creating itself. In Euripides' telling of a tale, one is reminded of how Thomas Mann's Joseph, in the last book of his great tetralogy, reveals to his brothers, with charming clairvoyance, that they are all characters in a story, thus indirectly recalling the Prelude to the whole series, with its bemused speculation on the timeless existence of a story within the infinite recesses of time. Coexistent contrarieties, maintained by a detached, unfaltering self-consciousness, unconcealedly timing and managing all, hold the key to the art of the ironic mode.

In the earlier known tragedies, the contrarieties are for the most part allowed simply to coexist. It has been argued back and forth whether certain plays of Euripides are genuine tragedies, but the quarrel is chiefly over words. It has been said that the high mimetic was the mode of tragedy, or of the Sophoclean variety, at least; but for our one word "tragedy" we are indebted to three poets who all wrote differently, and there is small profit in narrowing the term to exclude the ironic tragedy of the *Alcestis* and other Euripidean plays; or, for that matter, the low mimetic tragedy of *Death of a Salesman*. The term is most convenient if left without too rigorous definition; if we overdefine it, or abandon it in criticizing Euripides, we miss his purposive use of conventional elements, and lose ourselves in tragical-pastoral-comical labels, picked ad hoc and utterly beyond any definition.

In any case, no one has ever denied that the *Medea* and the *Hippolytus* deserve to be called tragedies, though their manner of handling myth is ironic to the full. It is hard to find the Jason of *Pythian* IV in Euripides' play of 431. The self-interested brute who confronts us is far more repellent than the feeble Admetus, and his residual tormented human feeling, if that is what reveals itself in the final scene, comes too late to make any vital difference to the picture of him already staged. Medea's character is something more to be expected of the witch of tradition, who had murdered her little brother and old Pelias by the agency of his own daughters, but it is given complication in the play by her tragedy as a mother, the murder of her children, and its attendant anguish. This domestic aspect was not prescribed: there was an alternative version in which Medea destroyed only the princess and her father, the children being killed by the Corinthians in retaliation. Euripides wanted the vision of shattered domesticity, which he emphasizes and renders immediate in the figures of the Nurse and the Pedagogue, not merely in order to dramatize the violence of conflicting emotions and the extremities of revenge, but also for a thematic reason. The barbaric Medea, wronged and isolated, at first cuts an almost superhuman figure, contrasting powerfully with the low-mimetic persons of her household and the passive chorus. Even the fact of her motherhood is given heroic or at least martial dimensions by her famous statement: "I would rather stand with spear and shield three times / Than bear one child" (250–251). But as the determination grows upon her to slay the children, she herself grows, ironically, more and more human; though the tenderer affections are destined to be defeated, they are given full measure, and we witness the ruination, not of a heroine, but of a woman. What emerges thereafter is neither human nor heroic, but daemonic. Aristotle took exception to Medea's departure in the suddenly appearing chariot of the Sun on grounds that it was inorganic; rather, from the thematic point of view it is inevitable. Medea had come from Colchis, a sorceress and a barbarian; her adventure with Jason had been one of love and married life in Greece, whose advantages are stressed in the play (536 ff); but neither Greece nor marriage had brought advantage to her, only a heartless betrayal. Her departure, in the end, though geographically for Athens, is spiritually a return to Colchis; she had tried to be human, but the human scene was wanting in humanity, and she reverts to the witch. The detached and harrowing vista of the close amounts to a dismissal of the human condition, with all its supposed amenities, and an assertion of uncontrollable, daemonic power.

The impact of the *Hippolytus* is not much more encouraging. It begins with uncontrollable power, in the apparition of Aphrodite in the prologue, and ends with an epiphany of Artemis, equally uncontrolled, and potentially just as cruel (1420 ff). Between these Olympian poles, the drama of two basically noble persons destroyed plays like a puppet show, save that the puppets are convincingly alive and appealing. Again,

two figures of lower social caste, the huntsman companion of Hippolytus and Phaedra's loyal but morally
shabby nurse, throw an instant, immediate light on the
principals, modifying them, while the Olympians dwarf
them. Euripides had no need to diminish them further,
to achieve his irony, as he had diminished Jason or
Admetus. It was enough to allow them the foregone,
vain struggle toward their opposed extremes of high-
mindedness, and let the end speak for itself. Phaedra's
resolve to die of her passion, rather than to gratify it,
crumbles, or is crumbled for her by the Nurse, and she
sinks to criminal libel; Hippolytus maintains, even to
the letter, his allegiance to purity in word and act, but is
equally ruined. Theseus, guilty of one furious but
understandable deed, is left to mourn both wife and son,
with the godly reproof ringing in his ears. Humanity
has failed again, but more beautifully; the insufferable
arrogance of the young hero's asceticism is forgotten in
the light of his tragic adherence to it, and Phaedra's
personal hurt, both at Hippolytus' contempt and her
own failure, is brought to bear too poignantly for simple
condemnation. Both pathetically resemble the two
deities who destroy them. The wide gulf between god
and mortal is nowhere in Greek literature more touch-
ingly envisioned than in the quiet finale. Artemis
approves her votary, but abandons him because he is
dying, and she cannot lend her immaculate presence
to death; Hippolytus, on the brink of fulfilling his
mortality, acknowledges the unscathed freedom of the
divine in words of tender sorrow, tinged faintly with
reproach: "You part with ease from our long fellow-
ship" (1441). Artemis is sorrowful too, but cannot weep
(1396 ff); rather, she plans revenge by destroying a
favorite of Aphrodite's (1420 ff). As in the *Iliad*, the
game of the immortals goes on; the mortal players die

of their parts. And yet, in the rhythm of this closing scene, there spreads a broad wake of compassion, embracing both the dying and the deathless; Artemis, despite herself, leaves with a slight stain of human anguish on her heavenly garments.

In its gentle handling of humanity the *Hippolytus* complements and balances the *Medea's* dismissal of it. Taken together, the two plays present two important Euripidean themes which, as we have seen, were to be dramatized in close juxtaposition later in the romances; the earlier play concentrates on violence with terrible insistence; the *Hippolytus*, coming not long after, centers around the idea of purity, particularly in the figure of the hero, whose conception of it is firm, if not wholly sympathetic. But Phaedra too strives for purity, while yearning for something that would destroy it. Perhaps in both their cases it is more a matter of innocence than of purity in the sense of wholeness; the narrowly sexual terms of the plot tend to obscure whatever wider implications may have been in Euripides' mind at this period. In any case, he did not suggest the outlines of any larger whole as yet, either in the characters or in their myth. Yet he seems to reach toward them in the aetiological passages near the end of both plays: Medea, as she passes from protagonist to *dea ex machina*, says she will found a cult—one which actually existed—in honor of the dead children; and Artemis prophesies the equally real cult of the martyred Hippolytus. Euripides, whose concern with the origins of cults and other aetiological matters appears at times to be little more than antiquarian, here seems to intend more. Aeschylus could see the foundation of a cult as a kind of seal of validity upon the achievements of a trilogy; Euripides, whose plays contained no such achievements, nonetheless may have felt in the establishment of a religious institution some hint of permanence arising out of the ruins of dramatic world upon world, as though his keenly felt lack of comprehensive, or comprehensible scheme drove him to grasp at straws. If tragic mythology could not be rounded out into any form of salvation, even of the austerely structural, moral kind that Sophocles erected, at least it might leave memorials. The *Medea* and *Hippolytus* end at the tombs of innocence; true purity, wholeness, and salvation were still to seek.

Of all poets, Euripides did not see life steadily, and his era provided him with little help in seeing it whole. In the earlier plays, his dramatic renderings of myth are partial, in the sense that his detachment permits him only selective scrutiny of the parts of what once was an indissoluble whole: he sees the crushed flower of Phaedra's chastity, and the bright splinters of Hippolytus' self-admiring mirror; upon them the divine framework closes in like the walls in *The Pit and the Pendulum*. He sees Medea's volcanic despair bursting out of all frameworks, or, in another mood, a puny Admetus reprieved from all experience by the prince of gods, the prince of heroes, and a queen among wives. He sees all the pieces, but their snagged edges resist compliance with a total picture, or even with each other. The first task of the ironic mode is to disintegrate, and the gods in these plays, even the *Medea* where they take no overt part, function as the executors of a design of wholesale dismemberment, if design that be, and are far removed from the stately shapes who in earlier days, and always in Sophocles, could lend the inclusive magnitude and symmetry of their contours to the most shattering actions. Even the arraignment of Zeus that closes Sophocles' bitterest play, the *Trachiniae,* has a grand, sweeping, and apocalyptic ring in comparison to the mean and paltry spite of Cypris as avouched by Artemis (*Hipp.* 1400).

Skepticism and fragmentation lay deep in the spirit of

the age, an age of intellectual enlightenment, political darkness, and war; an age that, far from having no mythology, was haunted by numberless little myths, mostly paranoid, myths of empire, myths of the threat of astronomy or new gods, rhetorical myths about panaceas such as oligarchy, panhellenism, or Persian gold, and whole clusters of myths surrounding Alcibiades, and of course Socrates. It was easy to gain a reputation for atheism in that era, and Euripides among others did, while the truly godless escaped; the beady eye, with its tunnel-vision, found a threat in every instance of nonconformity. Euripides was not an atheist; but so far, though nonconformist certainly, he was still too much of his age, too shrewd, and above all too honest to be able to command more than a partial gathering of threads from the great myths, overlaid as they now were by all the little ones. True myth adumbrates the life of the world, with men and the gods in it, functioning in their proper spheres, or perhaps transgressing them, but always illustrating them and reenacting them, as in the figures of a cosmic dance. Myth takes narrative form because it must include time, to be whole; but its ultimate shape is static. It requires collective affirmation by the community, and individual recreation by the poet. But the poet's task is made inordinately difficult when collective affirmation is in abeyance. The age, not Euripides, was godless; he and Sophocles faced the same problem, though with widely differing responses. In the abundance of his religious suffering and poetic intensity, Euripides strove, as poets do, for the myth of the life of the world, the myth of salvation, while all the little myths scattered his work with by-products easily mistaken for his purpose. But the full rondure was not yet in sight, and partial structures, if any, were the most that he could build. Master of diversity that he was, he tried all manner of approaches; he was even to try the heroic mold, only once, and then not with heroic satisfaction.

Most of the plays that survive from the next decade or so deal with war, or its aftermath, and probe less deeply into the mysterious possibilities of myth as such. No plays illustrate more sharply the fitful disjointedness of Euripides' dramaturgy, or the ironic shifts and ambivalences to which it was subject. One may perhaps regret the mixed process of chance and selection by which the *Heracleidae, Andromache, Hecuba,* and *Suppliants* were preserved, rather than works far more famous in their own time, such as the *Telephus* or the *Andromeda.* Yet these, together with the *Trojan Women,* supply some knowledge of Euripides' reaction to the great war that was in progress, and its effect on his poetic creativity. The two earlier ones have been usually read as propaganda, and there is certainly anti-Spartan sentiment expressed in both; yet it may be wondered whether Euripides was not always too many-sided ever to write straight propaganda, and whether these plays are not rather motley products of a lifelong attempt to see myth whole, an attempt outflanked by inherent contradictions seen all too clearly.

The *Heracleidae,* for instance, could almost have been a drama of deliverance: the motifs are there. The children of Heracles are rescued from the persecutor of their father, Eurystheus, by Iolaus, Heracles' nephew and old comrade, and the intervention of the Athenians led by the sons of Theseus. Here is Athens, in her favorite role of protectress of the suppliant, engaged against Peloponnesians, if not actual Spartans; to this extent, propaganda may be at work. So far too the play enacts a vindication of right and innocence over darker powers, with justice supported by the willing self-

sacrifice of Macaria, daughter of Heracles, and symbolized by the rejuvenation of old Iolaus in the battle (796).
Rejuvenation, as a triumph over time, is closely akin to
Return from the Dead, and indeed in the original myth,
Iolaus actually returned from the underworld to protect
the children and slay Eurystheus. Euripides is fond of
the theme: besides Alcestis, Iphigeneia and Menelaus
are both represented as figuratively returning from
death, and Creusa, on recovering Ion, cries out that the
long-dead Erechtheus "grows young again, and the
earthborn house no longer gazes into night" (*Ion* 1465
f). In the *Heracleidae*, the idea is also lyrically celebrated in the apotheosis of Heracles and his marriage
with Hebe, eternal youth (871 f, 910 ff).

Noble self-sacrifice, high-minded defense of a cause,
defeat of the tyrant and triumph of justice, rejuvenation
or return from the dead—all was at hand for a play of
redemption, save that Euripides chose a variant in
which Eurystheus was not slain in battle, but taken
prisoner and executed, with much gloating, by order
of Alcmena, over the protests of the Athenians. To
complicate matters further, Eurystheus, like Oedipus,
bequeaths his body to the Athenians as an eternal
blessing, in return for their attempt to defend him.
The propaganda has gotten hard to follow, but the
Euripidean schema, or anti-schema, is familiar. Revenge is too potent a motive throughout Euripides'
theater to be omitted here, in the context of war and
bitterness, and Alcmena's revenge is at once bitter and
understandable (981 f). It reduces her stature and totally
reverses the moral tenor of the play, but so be it; she
has gained the upper hand and will make unsparing use
of it. As for Eurystheus, his sudden access of ambiguity
seems to balance Alcmena in what might be called the
transformation by war, a process to be studied again

in the *Hecuba*. As the helpless Alcmena turns into a vengeful fury, the vicious Eurystheus acquires some of the grace of martyrdom, merely by virtue of being her victim, somewhat in the way the Aeschylean Agamemnon, once his blood is spilt, becomes a rallying point for justice, his crimes forgotten. "Such is the life of man as the day that Zeus brings on," said Homer. Moral fixity is nowhere in view; relative situation is all. Myth has not yet been seen as the life story of the world, but at most as the framework for separate life stories, not all edifying.

The *Andromache* is perhaps the least elevated work that has come down to us; ironical as it is, it offers little internal irony, and no ambiguity, of either character or event. The good characters, Andromache, her son Molossus, and Peleus, emerge in safety, while the Spartan Menelaus and his barren, hysterical daughter are baffled in their jealous efforts to destroy the captive Trojan princess and the boy she has borne to Neoptolemus. Orestes, also represented as thoroughly Spartan and a thug, arrives in time to carry off Hermione from her husband, who would have been justly angry, if Orestes had not murdered him. We never meet Neoptolemus, but he seems to belong to the "good" characters, and we never learn why Apollo abetted his assassination—a problem that also embarrassed Pindar. Strictly speaking, although Andromache's captivity and her future in Epirus as the mother of the Molossians belongs to tradition, and despite the struggle between good and evil, the play as it stands is not myth at all; even Orestes' murder of Neoptolemus represents only the bedraggled epilogue of Greek heroic saga. The play is a domestic triangle, quite on the low mimetic level, the homeliest work by a dramatist often criticized for homeliness. As such, it is lively, especially in the psychological study of the two women, and in the rough but humane outspokenness of the heroine's savior, old Peleus, in whom appear, once more, some signs of opportune, though undeveloped, rejuvenation (761 ff).

But Euripides deliberately, by touch after touch, keeps the tone low and intimate. Andromache in bonds is not shown as a proud, noble sufferer; she pleads for her life with desperate eloquence, using vivid rhythmic devices in her lines (387 ff), such as those that later make Iphigeneia's appeal to the chorus so vocally audible and touching (*Iph. T.* 1056 ff). We are even told, to keep us aware that she is just human, that the cords on her arms are unnecessarily tight and painful: "Did you think you were tying up a bull or a lion?" asks Peleus as he releases her (720). And as for what she says in her defense against Hermione's jealousy, not even Hector, long dead, is allowed to escape Euripides' ironic determination to reduce everybody. Homer would have read with some surprise of Andromache patiently suckling Hector's various illegitimate offspring. Nowhere in Euripides is the diminution of heroic stature so complete and wholesale. Even Thetis at the end speaks less like the mourning goddess of the *Iliad* than like a good wife consoling her husband after long absence. Euripides has seen his characters as what is left in the wake of the disintegrating force, war. The structure too is disjointed: Andromache's rescue and Hermione's repentant terror have nothing to do with each other, from the point of view of cause and effect. Menelaus' departure to subdue a rebellious city is absurdly adventitious, while the roles of Orestes and Neoptolemus are poorly developed. Yet in the very chaos of this melodrama may be seen an embryo of the world of tyche, techne, and divinity, the motivational triad of the romances: characters devise, the unexpected intervenes to save both women, the good and the bad, while one god, Apollo, promotes an unjust murder, to the moral revulsion of the messenger (1161 ff), and another, Thetis, brings a touch of bittersweet charis to the close. The forces are not yet knit into a tight dramatic structure, but they are traceable.

The disintegrating power of war is at work to the full in the *Hecuba*, though now its effect is seen in gradual process, and it is joined also by a force of opposite trend, the growth of spiritual nobility amid suffering. Euripides seems to have had a special love for youth, and a corresponding, though less consistent, suspicion of those who have lived through the abrasiveness of many years. Polyxena, lovely in her youth and purity, and her aged mother, in her moral decay, divide the action in a fashion that has sometimes led critics to regard it as two separate dramas. But it is quite single in effect, its upward and downward movements complementing each other, the one exalting human nature until the self all but escapes from the cycle of growth and dissolution, the other following that cycle, boring steadily deeper into the morass of psychic corruption where the self is swallowed up. Polyxena, sacrificed on the tomb of Achilles, cannot be called a real martyr, for she sustains no cause, as does Macaria. She is the victim of a cruel whim, and her death is a waste, but her steadfast integrity, symbolized in her injunction that no one touch her except with the sword (547 ff), creates a moral monument a little after the Sophoclean manner, something out of nothing. Perhaps her beauty, as she kneels to the stroke, is compared to a statue for more than aesthetic reasons (560 ff); certainly her mother's reflection on a noble nature's inviolability under misfortune implies as much (597 f). But, like Alcmena, who inverts the affirmative march of events in the *Heracleidae*,

Hecuba herself now unfolds the other, sadder, one might say more Euripidean, side of the story. The proud queen, who has just said that moral knowledge once gained is unfailing, now proceeds to a revenge on her son's murderer that is both morally and physically grotesque, though speciously grounded on *Nomos*, the law that guarantees religion and justice (799 ff). Her conspiracy to blind Polymestor and murder his children begins with her gaining the complicity of Agamemnon, in return for the sexual pleasure he derives from Cassandra; it ends with the prophecy that Hecuba will be metamorphosed into a red-eyed hound, mad and screaming. This finely wrought tragedy, deliberately inconclusive as are so many plays of Euripides, involves no evident workings of the gods, and tyche is barely mentioned (786). Built entirely out of human, or inhuman, action, it forms a kind of detached but passionate dialectic of war's grim soil, both as matrix of the spirit's rootless loftiness, and the charnel house of its decrepit end.

Far less shapely in design, and more pervasively ironical in its treatment of war, the *Suppliants* begins as if it were going to be a festival drama in honor of one of Athens' most famous exploits, the rescue of the bodies of the Seven against Thebes, and their burial at Eleusis. But after Theseus, the idealized and here incongruously democratic King of Athens, has adopted the cause of Adrastus, bidden defiance to tyrannical Thebes, and recovered the corpses, the heroic action is suddenly stunted and dispersed in three sensational scenes presenting a new perspective on what has happened and what is still to happen. Having brought the corpses, Theseus directs Adrastus to give an oration over them, but warns him not to make foolish, unverifiable remarks about who did bravely or who stood next to whom; battle is too busy a time to ascertain such things. This prescriptive speech, with its critique of funeral rhetoric, breaks the illusion with something of the force of a parabasis. It is not funny, but its peremptory tone implies, "Go ahead, talk; but don't make too much of a fool of yourself." Adrastus then delivers an astonishing eulogy of his fallen comrades. Traditionally, the Seven, especially Capaneus and Tydeus, were champions hewn out of the toughest, most ungovernable vein of the old heroic rock, and Aeschylus so represented them; but in Adrastus' eloquence, these ruffians become gentlemen of such statesmanship, moderation, and simplicity of life as to seem positively demure in their valor. This done, the pyres begin to blaze; Evadne, wife of Capaneus, commits suttee, and her aged father resolves on death by starvation. The mothers and children of the fallen then collect their bones, general mourning being punctuated by the sons' prayer to avenge their fathers, a prayer that will be fulfilled, according to Athena, who speaks the epilogue. The tenor of these three scenes is ironical and reckless, yet coolly contrived to bring into view the uncontrollable; cheap rhetoric, self-destruction, and revenge suddenly replace nobility and devotion to a cause as motive powers.

The *Suppliants* has been associated with the Peace of Nicias (421 B.C.), and also with the refusal of Thebes to allow burial to the Athenian dead after the Battle of Delium (424 B.C.). But neither of these possible connections explains why Euripides built his play as he did. If the *Hecuba* comprises two contrary movements within a single mythic frame, the *Suppliants* seems to have two frames, one of dubiously simulated gold, the other of shabby wood with the veneer peeling off; or perhaps the frame simply breaks two-thirds of the way through, and fragments of the design spill out. The fine old

Athenian legend would have made a good festival play, for the precinct of the Seven, mentioned by Athena (1211 f), was actually shown to visitors at Eleusis and could have been an aetiological point of reference for an affirmative achievement of order within a mythological archetype. But Euripides sees elements that will not join in such a picture, separate empirical realities that belong to the story but have yet to find the frame that will afford them due proportion and stance within a whole.

The *Trojan Women* of 415 B.C., one of the most telling antiwar plays ever written, exhibits the extreme of fragmentation on the one hand, in scene after scene of suffering intense to the point of dementia, and on the other a lyrical unity not found in earlier treatments of the theme of war. It is all sustained, high-pitched lament, without countermovement and without relief. With the exception of the inconclusive debate between Helen and Hecuba, there is no real conflict, no cause and effect; only a steady, disjunctive series of mounting horrors, culminating in the burial of a murdered infant and the burning of the desolated city. For once, Euripides did not try to see everything in two ways at once, but simply wrote an extended threnody of overwhelming power, which presents no dramaturgical problems because it is not really a drama at all.

The work of Euripides is so diversified that any classification of it rests uneasily. Four of the five dramas here hesitantly grouped as war plays, however, have an interesting feature in common, from the point of view of playmaking, and that is the nature of their peripeties. The *Trojan Women*, of course, has none. A potential one might have developed in the Helen scene, had Euripides chosen to let Hecuba win her case with Menelaus; but he did not, and the play remained within the bounds of its dark lyricism. Yet it might be noted that neither the *Medea* nor the *Hippolytus*, which are real dramas, has a peripety in the full meaning of the word, that is, reversal of fortune, or change in the direction of the action. In both, the action is already well on its charted way when the drama begins, and no further access of knowledge or entrance of a character is needed to change it, or indeed could change it. The questionable arrival of Aegeus in the *Medea* may be discounted, on grounds that the heroine's actions are not altered by it, but at most facilitated. The *Alcestis* has a peripety in the arrival of Heracles, and is therefore more conventional in structure, though the pervasive irony of the play is not directly connected with it.

But the *Heracleidae*, *Andromache*, *Hecuba*, and *Suppliants* all have peripeties, and of a kind unwitnessed before on the Attic stage. Peripety, as a rule, is a reversal that corresponds with the climax of an irony inherent in the dramatic situation from the start. In these war plays, however, the reversals are not reversals of plot; they are reversals of moral perspective that come from outside, rather than from any inherent, organic dynamics of the action such as would bring them about inevitably; they are arbitrarily imposed by the hand of the poet in order to evolve a counterpiece that somehow negates the first half of the play. Thus in the *Heracleidae*, Iolaus, supported by the Athenians, performs an act of deliverance by rescuing Heracles' children; but for Alcmena, whose entrance marks the turning point, the victory is incomplete without the morally gratuitous, and openly deplored, counteract of mortal vengeance on Eurystheus. In the *Andromache*, the heroine is similarly delivered by an aged hero from her jealous enemy; but Orestes enters to save the pusillanimous Hermione and murder her husband in the act of making his peace with Apollo in the Delphian shrine. In the *Hecuba* and the *Suppliants*, the reversal is not accompanied by any new character, but enacted by those already present; Hecuba's plight is aggravated by the finding of Polydorus' body, but this discovery, nothing new in kind, is merely a final straw to bring the queen to a breaking point whose possibility she had implicitly denied. The reversal in the *Suppliants* is the most arbitrary of all; there seems to be no assignable reason for it, save that it suited Euripides' dramatic intuition to offset the socially understandable defense of civilization by Theseus against the torrid spectacle of Adrastus' sham oratory, Evadne's delirium, and the next generation's cry for vengeance. If there is any connection between the two parts, it lies in Theseus' initial hesitation to take up Adrastus' cause, which struck him at the very first as less than righteous (185 ff); but the emphasis of the play as built falls on its jerky discontinuity, rather than on a consistently developed story or moral scheme. Euripides, not the myth, is in control.

This kind of dramatic structure—for it is structure and not the failure thereof—stands in strong contrast to the organic architecture of Sophocles' plays. The form of a Sophoclean tragedy, even in the plays so drearily misnamed diptychs, is periodic, its contours rounded to include actions and characters proportionably conceived, and duly subordinated to the whole. Like myth itself, it finds an inevitable place within its self-wrought limits for every element, however disruptive or violent; it admits nothing irrelevant, and omits nothing that conduces to its fullness of representation and symmetry of design. Its dynamics, including those of peripety, are wholly interior to the scheme; its voice is one of high decorum, both rich and economical, while its mode, the high mimetic, builds its rondure upon a heroic, vertical axis creating intension and unity.

The plays of Euripides so far have shown a very different pattern. It is as if, to continue the figure, the axis were horizontal, with implications of unlimited extension and scope, and the circumference sometimes lost beyond the horizon. Its ironic mode, tinctured with the low mimetic, admits dynamic influences from any source whatever, rather favoring those that come from outer chaos, and leaving their results for the most part unassimilated. As for what it chooses to represent, its concern is with parts in all their vividness, and it deliberately ignores whatever whole they may be thought to belong to. Symmetry is no object, but rather disparity, inconcinnity, and rough edges, in a perspective where no places are proper to the fragments in their eternal flux. The myth does not fulfill itself, for the spiritual periphery, whether belonging to men or gods, is lost, so that even the mythic frame, the phrase used above to denote a traditional story, becomes only an alien outline drawn by the arbitrary hand of the artist himself.

The result is a totally unperiodic form, paratactic and episodic, in which scene follows scene because it does, rather than because it must; in which even a character need have few, if any, inner springs of action. If Medea and Phaedra are three-dimensional, there are few figures in the war plays to be compared with them: Hecuba and Adrastus have rudimentary shading, but Theseus, Andromache, Iolaus, and Peleus are as paper-thin "good" characters, as Menelaus, Alcmena, Odysseus, and the Theban herald are "bad." The struggle between good and evil is melodramatically uncomplicated, not because Euripides, of all people, was unable to represent it otherwise, but because he chose this approach as suited to his detachment, and to his gift for clear delineation of parts, details, and fragments. In so choosing, he created an extremely productive medium, traceable through Seneca, the historical dramas of the

Elizabethans, and into the so-called "epic theater" of Brecht. *The Caucasian Chalk Circle* and *Mother Courage* probably have more of the artistic flavor of this phase of Euripides' work than any translations of him could convey.

Epic theater, though regular with Euripides in plays whose theme is war, does not by any means account for his formal repertoire in general. He was capable of a more coherent internal syntax and of a deeper involvement with character, as the *Electra* and *Heracles* both show. In the *Electra,* the mainspring of both action and character is revealed by that keen psychological perception for which Euripides has been justly celebrated; and the peripety, if such is the right name for the emotional collapse that overtakes the two principals at the end, comes about as the direct result of their warped criminal natures. For the poet has made clear that Orestes and his sister are criminal in spirit as in deed, in contrast to Sophocles' avenging pair, for whom the murder of Clytaemnestra and Aegisthus was a satisfying act of long-delayed justice. In contrast also with Aeschylus, for whom the traditional deed identified and determined the dramatic character, here, as in the *Orestes,* the deed rises out of a welter of psychic entanglement within the character; rather than simply attaching itself to the agent in the moment of the criminal act, the daemonic force is the product of the human soul, not, however, of a large, commanding soul, but of a mean one, grievance-laden and waveringly at odds with itself. Euripides has not lost his reductive irony. The heroic Orestes of the *Odyssey* has been replaced by an Orestes both stealthy and infirm of purpose, and Sophocles' strong-fibered, virgin witness-bearer by a small, hate-racked Electra, married to a dirt farmer, and piqued at her own deprivation. Euripides' rejection of any heroic treatment of the myth is pressed so far that his play has been thought a parody of Sophocles', and certain passages may actually be subtly parodic.

Yet, for all the dismissal of heroic dimensions, neither parody nor even irony accounts for the *Electra*, which seems to be an attempt to understand retribution not as justice, but as a morbid disorder of the mind. Euripides was wrestling frontally and effectively with one of the greatest archetypal myths, the myth of retribution, violence, and madness, whose themes pursued his imagination throughout his life. The factor of tyche is wholly absent, though that of techne, intrigue, is of course strong. The Dioscuri, who come to patch together some kind of orderly prospect for the guilty pair, and even mention Orestes' ultimate acquittal, can scarcely be said to stanch the engulfing misery of the close, or bring all into a rounded, divine perspective. But their assignment of responsibility to the oracle of Phoebus does not mean that Euripides is mounting an outspoken, total assault upon Apollo, as is so often said. All the Dioscuri say is that the exaction of justice is not necessarily a just deed, and that Apollo in his wisdom had enjoined what was unwise for them to perform (1244 f, 1301 f). As usual, Euripides has left the divine and the human in a state of unresolved paradox; divinity remains only vaguely concerned, the human agents suffer, and the framework of mythic wholeness is as incomplete as ever.

So is it also in the *Heracles*. In no other play did Euripides come so near to staging a genuinely heroic figure, or contrive a peripety so startling. The contest, as in the *Heracleidae*, is again over the children of Heracles, whom the tyrant Lycus wants to kill, along with their mother, lest they avenge his murder of their grandfather. They have taken refuge at an altar, for

Heracles is in Hades fetching the hound Cerberus, and is thought dead. Old Amphitryon alone clings to the hope of his return, but Megara prefers to abandon the altar and die with dignity, rather than be burned alive at it. Upon this scene of gloom, Heracles appears, rather like the rising sun, and kills Lycus. So far, the *Heracles* is a play of deliverance, built upon the myth of Return from the Dead. Despite the melodramatic pattern, the characters are given convincing roundness of life, especially Heracles, whose enduring greatness is movingly tempered with parental love. But this heartening picture is suddenly, hideously ruined. Lyssa, the spirit of raving madness, enters, reluctantly she says, but forced by the malevolence of Hera; the great, genial protector turns instantly maniac and slays the family that he has just rescued. In the messenger's appalling speech that describes the slaughter, Euripides spares no detail to make the reversal complete.

The murder of Megara and her children was one of the numberless traditional stories told about Heracles; it is an example of the contradictory criminal deed that so frequently occurs in the stories of great heroes. But it was Euripides' idea to put it immediately after the return from Hades, and no hint of motivation for this sudden access of madness can be found in the first part of the play. Unlike that of Orestes and Electra, the criminality of Heracles comes not from within but from without, and the goddess of unreason herself argues, most reasonably, against afflicting so good a man with so undeserved an evil (849 ff). It is the most telling instance of peripety imposed with external detachment by the playwright, such as was found in the war plays. But the *Heracles* is not confined by the circumstance of war; its reference is much wider, and the poet's irony seems applied directly to life itself. The myth of heroic salvation is shatteringly juxtaposed beside the myth of heroic destructiveness, to create a pageant of irrationality scarcely equaled even by the *Bacchae*. In the last scene Theseus, himself recently delivered from Hades by Heracles, enters to deter his benefactor from suicide, and to sustain him in bearing his grief. This lends a suggestion of trilogic synthesis to the foregoing thesis-antithesis; but one hears at most fragmentary, broken harmonies, and the end is muted more by despair than by true resolution.

But irony ultimately depletes itself, and a cloudlike detachment has a necessary kinship with cloudlike vision. Northrop Frye has noted how a recurrent cycle of modes can be discerned in the course of literary history. The mythic world of gods and cosmic heroes, created by early man, yields to the more sophisticated, though fabulous mode of the romantic mise-en-scène, a magical forest studded with mystic chapels and transforming fountains, peopled by puissant knights, sorcerers, and lovely damsels, and approximately limitless. Then, by a selective process, the scope is narrowed, the supernatural is confined or expelled, and the single great figure of the high mimetic mode stands forth. He is followed by the more general populace of the world, objectively and realistically envisioned in low mimetic colors; after which objectivity leads on to ever increasing detachment, and irony becomes the characteristic mode of literature. Then at a certain point a new cycle begins. The ironic mode, when exercised to the extreme, grows so remote from the immediacy of daily experience that the details become indistinct, leaving only broad outlines that presently begin to take on mythic shape, and to resemble once more primordial hypotheses of the totality of things. The direction is now diametrically away from the precision of the low mimetic and toward the large approximations of myth. Myth is reborn as a kind of order perceived in the residual, vague, and ironically distanced outlines of the world, an order that is the invention of the mind to be a stay against the threat of encroaching chaos, as what was formerly precise vision becomes attenuated and confused.

It is at this juncture of modes that we find the art of Euripides as he set about the composition of the *Iphigeneia*, *Helen*, and *Ion*. Partly as a result of the age in which he lived, and partly because of his own temperament, he had found irony a native element. But with the *Heracles* he reached a point beyond which he could not proceed without rediscovering what lay behind him, as if he were walking on the surface of a sphere. The extreme detachment of the *Heracles* betrays itself only with the entrance of Lyssa. Up till then, we have been beguiled into a high degree of emotional involvement with Heracles and his family; the cold horror of the reversal is a shock beyond description because it comes so totally from outside the dramatic texture, and shows us that we, like Megara and the children, have been mercilessly deceived, not by Heracles, but by the mindless, chaotic nature of existence. Irony could scarcely be carried farther, and Euripides, to our knowledge, never tried to do so. Instead he pushed on to something new, as was his habit, and it is not impossible that he was surprised to find himself rediscovering myth as a pattern of some kind of whole, arising out of the wisplike tatters of a world strewn across a steadily receding sky.

The intellect, or imagination, necessarily forms such patterns, though they shift and change with equal necessity. The extreme of irony must begin to recreate myth, because it is the basic function of the mind to create categories of the recognizable, to make ordered intelligibility out of the chaos of infinitely diverse experience;

and the more diverse and unintelligible experience is found to be, the more the mind must invent, if it is to transmit its findings. Chaos is incommunicable by the mind, except for the name, so that the most detached, honest, and complete acknowledgment of chaos is the most inevitably bound to create hypotheses of order as a recourse for communication. The only alternative would be silence, a kind of death of the world. Hence order is, one might say, a by-product of the mind compelled by chaos, a hypothesis; and a complete hypothesis of order is one definition of myth. Another definition, one that looks to its narrative aspect, is the story of the world's life, the mind's grasp of which becomes the *ver novum* in which the world is reborn in its visionary wholeness, with gods, men, and nature all performing their own interacting parts.

The story of the world's life is what Euripides seems to have come to in the *Iphigeneia* and its two companion works. In these as in no others he was content to let the full pattern of myth have its say, without diminution or distortion. He was able to do this not because of any "real" event, least of all because of any desire to escape from reality, but because he had traversed the full course of irony and brought a new reality into view, a more complete reality, and one that included salvation in its scope. No mystical insight, or dawn of hitherto unheard-of knowledge, was involved, but only the natural conclusion of one process and the beginning of another. Nor was he bound to the new process as to a newly revealed religion. These plays were not the end of his career, and he was to go on, once these were done, to write other and different works. Rather they marked a perception, momentary perhaps, but a perception appropriate to a phase, which had arisen inevitably out of the pursuit of his art, something which, like the clarity

and deliverance that the protagonists of these plays discover in their destinies, had been inherent from the first.
Euripides has been too much identified with the beginnings of philosophy, and not enough with the mythology
of the age and tradition in which he worked. It was not
philosophy that had made him an ironist to begin with,
but the unruly horde of ironies already existent in his
chosen form of tragedy as a world view. These gave birth
to partial and biased views of myth, but myth never
ceased to be the point of reference; it was both the
matrix and the prospective aim of tragedy to see a
mythic whole, and to embrace at least some glimpse of
order, however fleetingly. In the vision of these three
dramas, Euripides followed his myths to the brink of
their fullest import, and accepted the possibility of redemption as part of the complete tragic scope.

Before concluding his poem in the Euganean Hills,
Shelley wrote:

> Other flowering isles must be
> In the sea of life and agony.

We should have to possess Euripides' entire work in
order to know if his irony at other periods in his life led
him full circle to other flowering isles of healing myth;
but it seems to have done so once, at least. A better name
should be found for the romances, for though two of
them satisfy many of the requirements of Frye's romantic mode, the greatest of them, *Ion*, does not, and all
three imply more than the deep forest realm of haunted
spots and unlikely encounters, of magic and metamorphosis. In their outcomes, Euripides' unlikelihoods are
shown to be tokens of the inevitable, and metamorphosis, when it is operative as in the *Helen*, presents a
temporary obstruction certainly, but later a new phase

of reality; it is more like an Ovidian or Apuleian metamorphosis than those of Spenser's Angelica. The *Iphigeneia*, *Helen*, and *Ion* are bound together by something
more basic than the orientation of romance. Perhaps
they could be called the mythic plays, in the special
sense that in them a traditional story has been dramatized to attain a kind of wholeness, a totality in which
all external irony is suppressed or assimilated, and where
elements of romance, melodrama, and even depth psy-
chology may enter, but only to play contributory parts,
subsumed and adjusted to the larger controlling vision.
For the first time in Euripides' known work, the mythic
frame completes itself; the characters, too, complete
themselves by remaining within it and discovering
selves they had scarcely hoped they might possess. Iphigeneia, the victim, becomes her own and her brother's
savior, while he, the tainted fugitive, participates in the
act of salvation and becomes the rightful king of his
land. A phantom Helen, destroyer of men, is absorbed
into universal aether and replaced by the true and redemptive wife, no longer the antithesis of Penelope, but
her counterpart. Ion, the waif, finds himself the son of a
great god and father of the Ionian people; Creusa, who
believed herself to be Apollo's forgotten plaything, finds
herself a whole woman, suddenly numbered with the
ageless heroines.

These redemptions, though hard-won in the eleventh
hour, are far from the vulgar timely arrivals of a melodramatic or romantic hero. They are all recognitions of
truth built from within the plays themselves; they are
recognitions of others linked with self-recognition, and
dramatized through organic peripeties. The recognition
scene of the *Iphigeneia* is justly famous; the *Helen's* is
less vivid; but that of the *Ion* is perhaps the most beautiful, because of the powerful symbolism of integrity in

Creusa's crown of imperishable olive. No external irony can legitimately be read into these great moments of change, for their revelations are of inherent truth, like axioms rightly stated. They have also a touch of the apocalyptic in them, since they disclose the part played by divinities along with faceless chance and human choice, or contrivance, to form that triad of causation whose factors seem to work independently and as they please, but, when seen entire, in a kind of uncertain union. There is a hypothesis of wholeness in these three plays not found in any earlier ones, the wholeness of myth adumbrating human experience viewed whole.

Widely as the three stories differ, the underlying myth is the same for all three, and one that Euripides had made use of in two previous plays, the *Alcestis* and the *Heracles*. It is the great myth of Return from the Dead, which appears in numberless guises, the archetype in Greek literature being the *Odyssey*. Literal death is not necessary, nor is any doctrine of immortality involved. Odysseus does not literally die; he visits the land of the dead and returns, as do all heroes in one way or another. Part of the even larger myth of the hero, which is the world's life cycle seen in its individual aspect, this journey frames a metaphor of victory over death; it betokens the rounding of the cycle, as the Return of Persephone betokens vegetational rebirth. It is immaterial that for the fields rebirth is a fact, for the hero an aspiring venture of the mind; for the spirit conquers through the transmutation of experience, real or imagined, into knowledge. Knowledge is all that Odysseus brought home from his metaphoric journey, and it is the metaphor of rebirth, with access of true knowledge, that is woven into the fabric of these three plays. The spectators at Aulis witnessed the slaughter of Iphigeneia; Creusa with her own hands exposed her infant;

Menelaus was supposed dead, and the real Helen has been all but dead, save to herself, for many years (*Helen* 286). The great recognitions each mark the return of someone who has been lost; true knowledge supervenes, and the cycle is found complete. Iphigeneia and Orestes embrace with words expressive of new life (827 ff); the sepulchral music of the Sirens invoked by Helen is supplanted by the celebrant flutes and timbrels of the Great Mother (167 ff; 1346 ff); the house of Erechtheus is revived in Ion (1465 ff).

To what a different purpose had Euripides turned this myth in the *Alcestis* and the *Heracles!* Though both of those returns take place, neither brings about a vision of wholeness or of lasting salvation; Alcestis comes back an ironic ghost, a statue silently scanning a dramatic world void of spiritual stature; Heracles' return is that of a real hero, but its saving power is instantly annulled by a stroke of the cosmic Irrational that subverts his very essence. Euripides could not, or at least did not at that point, see any terminal of deliverance arising from heroic mythology. He took stories whose core was the defeat of death and all its dark powers, and denied them their inalienable right to triumphant music, in the one play by showing the world as morally dead, in the other by disallowing the possibility of meaningful salvation in a world of meaningless unreason. He had yet to give the myth its head and let it tell its story in full. Still, that mythic aspiration, the defeat of decay and death, haunted his creative process, and in two other plays, the *Andromache* and *Heracleidae*, he permitted the closely related motif of rejuvenation to hint at it. The rejuvenation of Iolaus is real, but its moral potential is left without direction, as the emphasis shifts to Alcmena's revenge. The restored youth of Peleus does, however, achieve the rescue of Andromache and, as we have seen, that play also moves by the same motive power, techne, tyche, daimon, that functions so intricately in the three "mythic plays." The *Andromache* is too haphazardly constructed and too lacking in unity to equal them in effect, but in this regard it may be seen as a precursor of their attainment of mythic and spiritual fullness.

It is a matter of taste whether or not one chooses to regard the achievement of the *Iphigeneia*, *Helen*, and *Ion* as the climax of Euripides' development. One might do so on the grounds that to include the possibility of salvation within the tragic scheme, as something, in fact, inherent to it, provides the act of synthesis that tragedy strives toward, an ulterior state of equilibrium that presumably was the regular keynote of the third play of an Aeschylean trilogy. Tragic action, so filled out, then corresponds to the full sweep of myth as principle of order and as the life history of the world. In his *Tragedy and Comedy*, Walter Kerr contends that tragedy, for all its mimesis of destruction, is in reality an affirmative statement of the human spirit; when enacted in its complete form, as in the trilogy, the tragic rhythm comprises action and suffering, followed by some manner of redemption, much as in Fergusson's formula: purpose, passion, perception. Plays of tragic flavor that do not include this third function are either only partial representations arising, one may suppose, from only partial envisionment of the tragic experience or, if full envisionments, ones in which the redemptive element is at most suggested in "continuing figures" like Horatio and Fortinbras in *Hamlet*, or motifs of permanence, such as the cults of Hippolytus or Medea's children. If that be true, Euripides' earlier works belong to the less complete category, while the mythic plays comprehend the whole tragic cycle. Evaluated in that light, they might be taken as a culminating point, something that the poet had been striving for and had at last achieved, a kind of artistic and philosophic completeness expressed in a drama rounded to fit the liberating wholeness of myth.

There is much to be said in favor of this view, but it calls for some caution. In the first place, it leaves out of account the last plays, or, worse, implies that they are to be reckoned as failures of the newly won completeness, and reversions to the more limited tragic outlook. Secondly, one might be misled into confusing the kind of wholeness found in Euripides' mythic plays with Sophocles' very different vision. The figure, earlier proposed, of the vertical versus the horizontal axis might be helpful here in drawing the distinction. Sophocles' vertical axis is abstracted from the spinal column of the hero, the central, indispensable figure of the high mimetic mode. Through choice, action in isolation, reversal and suffering, this figure is fleshed out in all its identity, both individual and representative, and given a moral stature comparable to the dynamic stature of the divine, so that the two stand in an indissoluble ontological union. This dramaturgy was called periodic because all its parts turn toward the center and are confined within the outlines of the dominating heroic figure; he (or she) is, in fact, the action, and nothing happens in the play that is not of this figure's own doing. Euripides never staged such a figure, or strove to; his art is not concerned with the ontology of the individual, nor is it markedly metaphysical, if at all. Though assuredly concerned with gods as well as men, its concern finds itself in jarring juxtapositions, spiked antitheses of action and personalities, dilemmas of belief or the lack of it. The axis of Euripidean drama lies in a horizontal plane of phenomenological experience, gathering within its sweep all the diversity of things in whatever disarray, and inciting them to react at will among themselves. Elements need not be organic to enter into Euripidean drama, which is collective rather than selective, and so nonperiodic that at times it resembles disorder, or even chaos itself. But if this horizontal axis be regarded as revolving, and its motion be produced to one full revolution, the circle so described will be complete, and everything collected within it will have a place, as in a myth seen whole.

The semblance of order thus captured will, however, be momentary, for the axis will continue its circuit and may stop anywhere. A culmination need not be the end, nor all that follows it a decline. Hence, if the subsequent plays differ from the mythic three, if the *Orestes* seems to resemble the *Electra*, and the *Phoenissae* brings back the epic theater of the war plays, they must not be regarded as retrogressions, but as part of a continuing process of dramaturgical gathering and observation. As for the *Bacchae*, with its unique staging of frontal conflict between a man and a god, and its universal vision of indiscriminate creation and indiscriminate wreckage, that is something new again, the world-imperiling drama where the ironical god of the Seventh Homeric Hymn plays the role of hero in the myth of his own triumph.

With these reservations in mind, then, it may be permissible to regard the mythic plays as a culmination. They do not, of course, constitute a rejection of earlier work, such as Yeats and other poets have voiced; but they are the only plays in the corpus that rely on their myths in their entirety, without either that kind of corrosive irony that imposes upon their action and forestalls its reaching a point of rest, or the kind that reduces the agents so completely that they no longer bear any relation, save a mocking one, to the heroic world where they were born. It is not that irony has disappeared;

Euripidean drama would be unthinkable without it. But it is more restrained; it appears chiefly in the familiar guise of internal, dramatic irony, which arises out of the plot and emerges in speeches implying more than the character knows, or foreshadowing what the audience has yet to learn. For the rest, the poet's own irony is evident in the general conception, but it plays with forbearance over the characters and the texture of the language, making the young Ion believe quite easily that Erichthonius was born out of the earth, but causing the sophisticated Helen to wonder, in a troubled way, about her own origin in an egg.

It is a serious error to inflate these and other delicate touches of humor, such as the mental limitations of Xuthus and Menelaus, to the extent of turning the plays into comedies. In all three there is only one line that really breaks the dramatic illusion (*Helen* 1056), and the main characters, though lacking the monolithic greatness of Sophoclean heroes, all have a genuine dignity that enforces their serious acceptance. The protagonists are not quite high mimetic, but they are not low mimetic either; they are ironic figures moving homeward into myth. All are compounded of small and large, of helplessness and strength. Iphigeneia is a blend of girlishness and self-sacrificial power; Ion is a boy germinating the seeds of heroism; Helen, destroyer and destroyed, preserves herself and her husband. Creusa, the fullest and loveliest portrait of a woman in all Euripides, relives the shock and terror of a violated girl under her queenly poise. With restrained and tender hand, Euripides has allowed them all to complete themselves as the myth foresaw them.

One is not surprised to find that the women in these plays are more impressive than the men, who waver and fumble; but that fact does not make Euripides a feminist, any more than certain glib, derogatory remarks from various characters—often female—make him a misogynist. Society has always enjoyed formulating and attributing vulgar generalities about women, and since neither label fit Euripides, he has been awarded both. A better answer might be found in the kind of artistic venture that the poet has in hand. If the women of the mythic plays wear the mantle of the *Ewig-weibliche* and surpass the men, it is perhaps because in this context woman, like myth, is looked upon as peculiarly able to contain and hold in suspension all manner of contradictory influences and equivocal signs until their equipoise is reached. Again, Creusa offers the most moving example; until the very end she remains thoroughly ambiguous in her feelings toward Apollo, never forgiving his treatment of her, yet never quite abandoning her hope in him. The myth is Creusa; its completion is her completion, and by implication the world's.

Perhaps the real question is not, how Euripides came to write the way he did around 412 B.C., but why he never wrote that way before, or for that matter, afterwards. That question is simply not answerable. Without a reliable biography, we cannot ascertain what influences were brought to bear upon the formation of his poetic gift, so that it emerged in such contrast with Sophocles'. Possibly the slight difference in their ages was made more significant by the fact that Sophocles grew up in the heady days of the Persian Wars, while Euripides did not have those heroic paradigms at first hand in his memory. Possibly too his outlook on myth was affected by what is vaguely called the decline of religion in the later fifth century, under the pressure of the Sophistic Enlightenment. The second answer, though honored by time, is specious, for poets do not work pri-

marily with concepts nor are they mere products of a
Zeitgeist. After all, Sophocles also felt the impact of the
Enlightenment and reacted with quite a different kind
of tragic art. But ever since his own day it has been common practice to put Euripides into strained religious
postures, and make him an apostate from religion and
myth. It seems more true to say that he was probing for
the meaning of myth, as all his predecessors had done,
and finding it in his own way.

As for his rejecting religion, it is hard to explain that
judgment upon a poet so obviously religious as Euripides. The assumption seems to be that he could not put
faith in gods who behaved as badly as the Olympians
did. But the Olympians did not require faith, they re-
quired observance, and by Euripides' day they must have
been used to complaints about their morals; they had
been hearing a good many since the days of Xenophanes,
and probably before. Such moral diatribes were hack-
neyed quibbles by Euripides' time, and if some of his
characters, in moments of stress or puzzlement, felt
driven to repeat them, the community of Olympians
may have listened with some boredom, but we should
credit them with the intelligence not to mistake a stage
persona for the poet's own, as so many critics have
done. It is hard to say which is more naive, to imagine,
with Verrall, a philosopher of the stage who devoted his
life work to deriding the gods with complacent cyni-
cism, in protest against a blind faith that nobody ever
entertained, or to see him, as some more recently have
done, as an apologist for the inherited religion trying to
show how the gods do all for the best. If Apollo in the
Ion does not live up to quite all the worst fears expressed about him, his image must not therefore be
tortured into embracing all the providential benignity

ever piously hoped for in a deity. What he did live up to was a quite familiar Olympian standard.

Euripides' ideas about the gods were probably as unsteady as most of his contemporaries'. He often represented the universe as alien and cruel, the gods included. For the gods, though mightier and longer-sighted than mortals, provide only a partial understanding of ultimate mysteries. Men and gods alike are figures in a myth, which alone presumes to embrace those mysteries, and in the *Iphigeneia*, *Helen*, and *Ion* Euripides appears to have tested its claim fully for the first time. It was not a case of the ironic poet's escaping from the bitterness of his own irony into a world of half-comic romance; his own irony had led him back to myth by the long route. Myth arrived at in this way differs in tone from the pristine myth of society in its formative stage, but it has the same qualities of self-completeness and approximation of order. Yet all myth, whether pristine or recovered, speaks less in the voice of conviction than of aspiration, and such is Euripides' mood here. His task as a tragic poet was to find adequate framework for his vision of the world about him, and the conventions of tragic form provided him with the infinite, demiurgic wealth of mythology. Much of the time he had found only parts of the structure to his purpose, but at the period in question he must have seen myth as a tentative hypothesis of wholeness, a hypothesis that reaches out and, after crucial effort, waiting, and confusion, comprehends a kind of redemptive fulfillment that exists for man only as he and the myth coexist and reach their completeness together. As the sweep hand of the tale comes round, things that had been thought to have perished are rediscovered in all their purity, and in Pindar's words, "A bright glow is upon man, and his life is sweet." The profound seriousness of the mythic dramas has been too long obscured by the lightness of their creator's touch. Creusa's crown of olive does not belong in the lost-and-found department of New Comedy; it belongs with the anonymous poet's Pearl.

Selected
Bibliography

Bowra, Sir C. M., *The Greek Experience*, Cleveland, 1957
Burnett, Anne Pippin, *Catastrophe Survived*, Oxford, 1971
[———], ——— "Euripides' *Helen*: A Comedy of Ideas," *Classical Philology* 55 (1960), 151 ff
Conacher, D. J., *Euripidean Drama: Myth, Theme, and Structure*, Toronto, 1967
Dale, A. M., ed., *Helen*, Oxford, 1967
Dodds, E. R., ed., *Euripides: Bacchae*, Oxford, 1944
Edmunds, A. Lowell, *Chance and Intelligence in Thucydides*, Cambridge, Mass., 1974
Else, G. F., *Aristotle's Poetics: The Argument*, Cambridge, Mass., 1957
Frye, Northrop, *Anatomy of Criticism*, Princeton, 1957
Grube, G. M. A., *The Drama of Euripides*, London, 1941
Harrison, Jane, *Prolegomena to Greek Religion*, Cambridge, 1903
Kannicht, R., *Euripides, Helena*, Heidelberg, 1969
Kerr, Walter, *Tragedy and Comedy*, New York, 1957
Kitto, H. D. F., *Greek Drama*, Doubleday Anchor Books, New York, 1955
Knox, B. M. W., "Euripidean Comedy," in *The Rarer Action: Essays in Honor of Francis Fergusson*, New Brunswick, 1971
——— "New Perspectives in Euripidean Criticism," *Classical Philology* 67 (1972), 270 ff
Lesky, A., *Greek Tragedy*, trans. H. A. Frankfort, London, 1965
Murray, Gilbert, *Euripides and His Age*, Cambridge, Mass., 1913
Norwood, Gilbert, *Greek Tragedy*, Boston, 1920
Owen, A. S., ed., *Ion*, Oxford, 1939
Pearson, A. C., ed., *Euripides: Helena*, Cambridge, 1903
Platnauer, M., ed., *Iphigenia in Tauris*, Oxford, 1938

Renehan, R., *Greek Textual Criticism*, Cambridge, Mass., 1969

Segal, Charles P., "The Two Worlds of Euripides' *Helen*," *TAPA* 102 (1971), 553 ff

Solmsen, F., "*Onoma* and *Pragma* in Euripides' *Helen*," *Classical Review* 48 (1934), 119 f

Verrall, A. W., "Euripides' Apology (Helen)," *Essays on Four Plays of Euripides*, Cambridge, 1905

Wecklein, N., ed., *Euripides: Ausgewählte Tragödien*, Leipzig, 1880

——— *Euripides: Helena*, Leipzig, 1907

Wolff, Christian, "Design and Myth in Euripides' *Ion*," *Harvard Studies in Classical Philology* 69 (1965), 169 ff

Zuntz, Gunther, *An Inquiry into the Transmission of the Plays of Euripides*, Cambridge, 1965

——— "On Euripides' *Helena*: Theology and Irony," *Entretiens Fondation Hardt* VI, Geneva, 1960, 201 ff

——— *The Political Plays of Euripides*, Manchester, 1955